# Blood Brothers

## A Musical

## book, music and lyrics by
## Willy Russell

A SAMUEL FRENCH ACTING EDITION

FOUNDED 1830

SAMUELFRENCH.COM
SAMUELFRENCH-LONDON.CO.UK

ISBN 978-0-573-08064-7

www.SamuelFrench.com

www.SamuelFrench-London.co.uk

## FOR PRODUCTION ENQUIRIES

### UNITED STATES AND CANADA
Info@SamuelFrench.com
1-866-598-8449

### UNITED KINGDOM AND EUROPE
Plays@SamuelFrench-London.co.uk
020-7255-4302/01

Each title is subject to availability from Samuel French, depending upon country of performance. Please be aware that *BLOOD BROTHERS* may not be licensed by Samuel French in your territory. Professional and amateur producers should contact the nearest Samuel French office or licensing partner to verify availability.

## MUSIC USE NOTE

Licensees are solely responsible for obtaining formal written permission from copyright owners to use copyrighted music in the performance of this play and are strongly cautioned to do so. If no such permission is obtained by the licensee, then the licensee must use only original music that the licensee owns and controls. Licensees are solely responsible and liable for all music clearances and shall indemnify the copyright owners of the play(s) and their licensing agent, Samuel French, against any costs, expenses, losses and liabilities arising from the use of music by licensees. Please contact the appropriate music licensing authority in your territory for the rights to any incidental music.

## IMPORTANT BILLING AND CREDIT REQUIREMENTS

If you have obtained performance rights to this title, please refer to your licensing agreement for important billing and credit requirements.

# BLOOD BROTHERS

First performed at the Liverpool Playhouse on 8th January, 1983, with the following cast:

| | |
|---|---|
| **Mrs Johnstone** (Mother) | Barbara Dickson |
| **Mickey** | George Costigan |
| **Eddie** | Andrew C. Wadsworth |
| **Sammy** | Peter Christian |
| **Linda** | Amanda York |
| **Mrs Lyons** | Wendy Murray |
| **Mr Lyons** | Alan Leith |
| **Narrator** | Andrew Schofield |
| **Chorus** | Hazel Ellerby |
| | Eithne Brown |
| | David Edge |

Directed by **Chris Bond**
Designed by **Andy Greenfield**
Musical Director **Peter Filleul**
(Presented by arrangement with **Bob Swash**)

Subsequently presented by Bob Swash, by arrangement with Liverpool Playhouse at the Lyric Theatre, London, on 11th April, 1983, with the following cast:

| | |
|---|---|
| **Mrs Johnstone** (Mother) | Barbara Dickson |
| **Mickey** | George Costigan |
| **Eddie** | Andrew C. Wadsworth |
| **Sammy** | Peter Christian |
| **Linda** | Kate Fitzgerald |
| **Mrs Lyons** | Wendy Murray |
| **Mr Lyons** | Alan Leith |
| **Narrator** | Andrew Schofield |
| **Chorus** | Hazel Ellerby |
| | David Edge |
| | Ian Burns |
| | Oliver Beamish |

Directed by **Chris Bond** and **Danny Hiller**
Designed by **Andy Greenfield**
Musical Director **Richard Spanswick**

# CHARACTERS

**Mrs Johnstone** (Mother)
**Narrator** (also appears as Milkman 1; Gynaecologist;
 Bus Conductor; Milkman 2; Teacher; rifle range man
**Mrs Lyons**
**Catalogue Man**
**Finance Man**
**Mr Lyons**
**Mickey** (ages from 7 to 20s)
**Edward** (ages from 7 to 20s)
**Sammy** (ages from 9 to 20s)
**Linda** (ages from 7 to 20s)
**Policeman**

Children, policemen, neighbours, wedding guests,
doleites, councillors, nurses, Judge

# MUSICAL NUMBERS

## ACT I

Music

| | |
|---|---|
| 1 | Overture |
| 2 | **Marilyn Monroe** (1) |
| 2(a) | **Marilyn Monroe** (reprise) |
| 3 | Underscoring |
| 4 | Underscoring |
| 5 | Underscoring |
| 6 | **My Child** |
| 7 | Underscoring |
| 8 | Underscoring |
| 9 | **Easy Terms** |
| 10 | Underscoring |
| 11 | **Shoes Upon The Table** (1) |
| 12 | **Easy Terms** (reprise) |
| | Doorbell |
| 13 | **Kids Game** |
| 14 | Underscoring |
| 15 | **Shoes Upon the Table** (2a) |
| 16 | **Shoes Upon the Table** (2b) |
| 17 | **Bright New Day** (preview) |
| 18 | **Long Sunday Afternoon** |
| 19 | **Bright New Day** |

## ACT II

| | |
|---|---|
| 20 | **Marilyn Monroe** (2) |
| | Car horn |
| 21 | Underscoring |
| 22 | Underscoring |
| 23 | Underscoring |
| 24 | Underscoring and **Shoes Upon the Table** (3a) |
| 25 | Underscoring |
| 26 | **That Guy** |
| 27 | **Shoes Upon The Table** (3b) |
| 28 | Underscoring |
| 29 | Underscoring |
| 30 | **I'm Not Saying A Word** |
| 31 | Underscoring |

The Music for this play is available on hire from Samuel French Ltd

# PRODUCTION NOTE

The setting for *Blood Brothers* is an open stage, with the different settings and time spans being indicated by lighting changes, with the minimum of properties and furniture. The whole play should flow along easily and smoothly, with no cumbersome scene changes. Two areas are semi-permanent—the Lyons house UL and the Johnstone house DR. We see the interior of the Lyons' comfortable home but usually only the exterior front door of the Johnstone house, with the "interior" scenes taking place outside the door. The area between the two houses acts as communal ground for street scenes, park scenes etc.

*Blood Brothers* is a rags-to-riches story that makes a haunting musical tragedy of our times. Mrs Johnstone, deserted by her husband and with a houseful of kids to feed, learns she is expecting twins, whom she cannot possibly afford to keep. She chars for childless Mrs Lyons who, learning of her plight, begs one of her twins from her at birth. The two boys grow up streets apart, never learning the truth but becoming firm friends (and in love with the same girl) despite their differing backgrounds and the attempts of Mrs Lyons to keep them apart. Mickey Johnstone loses his job, marries the girl, turns to crime and becomes dependant on tranquilisers. Edward Lyons prospers, goes to university and turns Councillor. But a Narrator, intruding like Fate, warns that a "price has to be paid". The price is the life of the blood brothers who die — Edward at the hands of Mickey, and Mickey at the hands of the police — fulfilling the prophecy that twins parted at birth will die on the day they find out their heritage.

# ACT I

## Music 1: Overture

*The Overture comes to a close*

**Mrs Johnstone**    Tell me it's not true
*(singing; off)*    Say it's just a story.

*The Narrator steps forward in a spotlight*

**Narrator**    So did y' hear the story of the Johnstone twins?
*(speaking)*    As like each other as two new pins,
Of one womb born, on the self same day,
How one was kept and one given away?

An' did you never hear how the Johnstones died,
Never knowing that they shared one name,
Till the day they died, when a mother cried
My own dear sons lie slain.

*The Lights come up to show a re-enactment of the final moments of the play—the deaths of Mickey and Edward (page 69). The scene fades*

*Mrs Johnstone enters with her back to the audience*

An' did y' never hear of the mother, so cruel,
There's a stone in place of her heart?
Then bring her on and come judge for yourselves
How she came to play this part.

*The Narrator exits*

*As the introduction to Music 1 is heard Mrs Johnstone turns and walks towards us. She is aged thirty but looks more like fifty*

## Music 2: Marilyn Monroe (1)

**Mrs Johnstone**    Once I had a husband,
*(singing)*    You know the sort of chap,
I met him at a dance and how he came on with the chat.
He said my eyes were deep blue pools,
My skin as soft as snow,
He told me I was sexier than Marilyn Monroe.

And we went dancing,
We went dancing.

Then, of course, I found
That I was six weeks overdue.
We got married at the registry an' then we had a "do".
We all had curly salmon sandwiches,
An' how the ale did flow,
They said the bride was lovelier than Marilyn Monroe.

And we went dancing,
Yes, we went dancing.

Then the baby came along,
We called him Darren Wayne,
Then three months on I found that I was in the club
    again.
An' though I still fancied dancing,
My husband wouldn't go,
With a wife he said was twice the size of Marilyn
    Monroe.

No more dancing
No more dancing.

By the time I was twenty-five,
I looked like forty-two,
With seven hungry mouths to feed and one more nearly
    due.
Me husband, he'd walked out on me,
A month or two ago,
For a girl they say who looks a bit like Marilyn Monroe.

And they go dancing
They go dancing

Yes they go dancing
They go . . .

*An irate Milkman (the Narrator) rushes in to rudely interrupt the song*

**Milkman** Listen love, I'm up to here with hard luck stories; you owe me
three pounds, seventeen and fourpence an' either you pay up today, like
now, or I'll be forced to cut off your deliveries.

**Mrs Johnstone** I said, I said, look, next week I'll pay y' . . .

**Milkman** Next week, next week! Next week never arrives around here. I'd
be a rich man if next week ever came.

**Mrs Johnstone** But look, look, I start a job next week. I'll have money
comin' in an' I'll be able to pay y'. Y' can't stop the milk. I need the milk.
I'm pregnant.

**Milkman** Well, don't look at me, love. I might be a milkman but it's got nothin' to do with me. Now you've been told, no money, no milk.

*The Milkman exits*

*Mrs Johnstone stands alone and we hear some of her kids, off*

**Kid One** (*off*) Mam, Mam the baby's cryin'. He wants his bottle. Where's the milk?
**Kid Two** (*off*) 'Ey Mam, how come I'm on free dinners? All the other kids laugh at me.
**Kid Three** (*off*) 'Ey Mother, I'm starvin' an ther's nothin' in. There never bloody well is.
**Mrs Johnstone** (*perfunctorily*) Don't swear, I've told y'.
**Kid Four**(*off*) Mum, I can't sleep, I'm hungry, I'm starvin'. . . .
**Kids** (*off*) An' me, Mam. An' me. An' me.

### Music 2A: Marilyn Monroe (reprise)

| | |
|---|---|
| **Mrs Johnstone** | I know it's hard on all you kids, |
| (*singing*) | But try and get some sleep. |
| | Next week I'll be earnin', |
| | We'll have loads of things to eat, |
| | We'll have ham, an' jam, an' spam an' |

(*Speaking*) Roast Beef, Yorkshire Puddin', Battenberg Cake, Chicken an' Chips, Corned Beef, Sausages, Treacle Tart, Mince an' Spuds, Milk Shake Mix for the Baby:

*There is a chorus of groaning ecstasy from the kids*

*Mrs Johnstone picks up the tune again*

> When I bring home the dough,
> We'll live like kings, like bright young things,
> Like Marilyn Monroe.

> And we'll go dancing . . .

*Mrs Johnstone hums a few bars of the song, and dances a few steps, as she makes her way to her place of work—Mrs Lyons' house. During the dance she acquires a brush, dusters and a mop bucket*

*The Lights crossfade to Mrs Lyons' house where Mrs Johnstone is seen working*

*Mrs Lyons enters, carrying a parcel containing new shoes*

**Mrs Lyons** Hello, Mrs Johnstone, how are you? Is the job working out all right for you?
**Mrs Johnstone** It's, erm, great. Thank you. It's such a lovely house it's a pleasure to clean it.
**Mrs Lyons** It's a pretty house isn't it? It's a pity it's so big. I'm finding it rather large at present.

**Mrs Johnstone** Oh. Yeh. With Mr Lyons being away an' that? When does he come back, Mrs Lyons?

**Mrs Lyons** Oh, it seems such a long time. The Company sent him out there for nine months, so, what's that, he'll be back in about five months' time.

**Mrs Johnstone** Ah, you'll be glad when he's back won't you? The house won't feel so empty then, will it?

*Mrs Lyons begins to unwrap her parcel*

**Mrs Lyons** Actually, Mrs J, we bought such a large house for the—for the children—we thought children would come along.

**Mrs Johnstone** Well y' might still be able to . . .

**Mrs Lyons** No, I'm afraid . . . We've been trying for such a long time now . . . I wanted to adopt but . . . Mr Lyons is . . . well he says he wanted his own son, not somebody else's. Myself, I believe that an adopted child can become one's own.

**Mrs Johnstone** Ah yeh . . . yeh. Ey, it's weird though, isn't it. Here's you can't have kids, an' me, I can't stop havin' them. Me husband used to say that all we had to do was shake hands and I'd be in the club. He must have shook hands with me before he left. I'm havin' another one y' know.

**Mrs Lyons** Oh, I see . . .

**Mrs Johnstone** Oh but look, look it's all right, Mrs Lyons, I'll still be able to do me work. Havin' babies, it's like clockwork to me. I'm back on me feet an' workin' the next day y' know. If I have this one at the weekend I won't even need to take one day off. I love this job, y'know. We can just manage to get by now——

*She is stopped by Mrs Lyons putting the contents of the package, a pair of new shoes, on to the table*

Jesus Christ, Mrs Lyons, what are y' trying to do?

**Mrs Lyons** My God, what's wrong?

**Mrs Johnstone** The shoes . . . the shoes. . . .

**Mrs Lyons** Pardon?

**Mrs Johnstone** New shoes on the table, take them off . . .

*Mrs Lyons does so*

(*Relieved*) Oh God, Mrs Lyons, never put new shoes on a table . . . You never know what'll happen.

**Mrs Lyons** (*twigging it; laughing*) Oh . . . you mean you're superstitious?

**Mrs Johnstone** No, but you never put new shoes on the table.

**Mrs Lyons** Oh go on with you. Look, if it will make you any happier I'll put them away . . .

*Mrs Lyons exits with the shoes*

**Music 3: Underscoring**

*Mrs Johnstone warily approaches the table*

*The Narrator enters*

**Narrator**         There's shoes upon the table an' a joker in the pack,
                     The salt's been spilled and a looking glass cracked,
                     There's one lone magpie overhead.
**Mrs Johnstone** I'm not superstitious.
**Narrator**         The Mother said
**Mrs Johnstone** I'm not superstitious
**Narrator**         The Mother said.

*The Narrator exits to re-enter as a Gynaecologist*

**Mrs Johnstone** What are you doin' here? The milk bill's not due 'till Thursday.
**Gynaecologist** (*producing a listening funnel*) Actually I've given up the milk round and gone into medicine. I'm your gynaecologist. (*He begins to examine her*) OK, Mummy, let's have a little listen to the baby's ticker, shall we?
**Mrs Johnstone** I was dead worried about havin' another baby, you know, Doctor. I didn't see how we were gonna manage with another mouth to feed. But now I've got me a little job we'll be OK. If I'm careful we can just scrape by, even with another mouth to feed

*The Gynaecologist completes his examination*

**Gynaecologist** Mouths, Mummy.
**Mrs Johnstone** What?
**Gynaecologist** Plural, Mrs Johnstone. Mouths to feed. You're expecting twins. Congratulations. And the next one please, Nurse.

*The Gynaecologist exits*

### Music 4: Underscoring

*Mrs Johnstone, numbed by the news, moves back to her work, dusting the table upon which the shoes had been placed*

*Mrs Lyons enters*

**Mrs Lyons** Hello, Mrs J. How are you?

*There is no reply*

(*Registering the silence*) Mrs J? Anything wrong?
**Mrs Johnstone** I had it all worked out.
**Mrs Lyons** What's the matter?
**Mrs Johnstone** We were just getting straight.
**Mrs Lyons** Why don't you sit down.
**Mrs Johnstone** With one more baby we could have managed. But not with two. The Welfare have already been on to me. They say I'm incapable of controllin' the kids I've already got. They say I should put some of them into care. But I won't. I love them. I love the bones of every one of them. I'll even love these two when they come along. But like they say at the Welfare, kids can't live on love alone.
**Mrs Lyons** Twins? You're expecting twins?

**Music 5: Underscoring**

*The Narrator enters*

**Narrator**          How quickly an idea, planted, can
                      Take root and grow into a plan.
                      The thought conceived in this very room
                      Grew as surely as a seed, in a mother's womb.

*The Narrator exits*

**Mrs Lyons** (*almost inaudibly*) Give one to me.
**Mrs Johnstone** What?
**Mrs Lyons** (*containing her excitement*) Give one of them to me.
**Mrs Johnstone** Give one to you?
**Mrs Lyons** Yes . . . yes.
**Mrs Johnstone** (*taking it almost as a joke*) But y' can't just . . .
**Mrs Lyons** When are you due?
**Mrs Johnstone** Erm, well about . . . Oh, but Mrs . . .
**Mrs Lyons** Quickly, quickly tell me . . . when are you due?
**Mrs Johnstone** July he said, the beginning of . . .
**Mrs Lyons** July . . . and my husband doesn't get back until, the middle of
    July. He need never guess . . .
**Mrs Johnstone** (*amused*) Oh, it's mad . . .
**Mrs Lyons** I know, it is. It's mad . . . but it's wonderful, it's perfect. Look,
    look, you're what, four months pregnant, but you're only just beginning
    to show . . . so, so I'm four months pregnant and I'm only just beginning
    to show. (*She grabs a cushion and arranges it beneath her dress*) Look,
    look. I could have got pregnant just before he went away. But I didn't tell
    him in case I miscarried, I didn't want to worry him whilst he was away.
    But when he arrives home I tell him we were wrong, the doctors were
    wrong. I have a baby, our baby. Mrs Johnstone, it will work, it will if only
    you'll . . .
**Mrs Johnstone** Oh, Mrs Lyons, you can't be serious.
**Mrs Lyons** You said yourself, you said you had too many children already.
**Mrs Johnstone** Yeh, but I don't know if I wanna give one away.
**Mrs Lyons** Already you're being threatened by the Welfare people. Mrs
    Johnstone, with two more children how can you possibly avoid some of
    them being put into care. Surely, Mrs Johnstone, surely it's better to give
    one child to me. Look, at least if the child was with me you'd be able to
    see him every day, as you came to work.

*Mrs Lyons stares at Mrs Johnstone, willing her to agree*

Please, Mrs Johnstone. Please
**Mrs Johnstone** Are y' . . . are y' that desperate to have a baby?

**Music 6: My Child**

**Mrs Lyons**          Each day I look out from this window,
(*singing*)            I see him with his friends, I hear him call,
                       I rush down but as I fold my arms around him,
                       He's gone. Was he ever there at all?

> I've dreamed of all the places I would take him,
> The games we'd play the stories I would tell,
> The jokes we'd share, the clothing I would make him,
> I reach out. But as I do. He fades away.

*The melody shifts into that of Mrs Johnstone who is looking at Mrs Lyons, feeling for her. Mrs Lyons, gives a half smile and a shrug, perhaps slightly embarrassed at what she has revealed. Mrs Johnstone, turns and looks at the room she is in. Looking up in awe at the comparative opulence and ease of the place. Tentatively and wondering she sings*

**Mrs Johnstone**        If my child was raised
                In a palace like this one,
                (He) wouldn't have to worry where
                His next meal was comin' from.
                His clothing would be (supplied by)
                George Henry Lee

*Mrs Lyons sees that Mrs Johnstone might be persuaded*

**Mrs Lyons**            He'd have all his own toys
    (*singing*)          And a garden to play in.
**Mrs Johnstone**        He could make too much noise
                Without the neighbours complainin'.
**Mrs Lyons**            Silver trays to take meals on
**Mrs Johnstone**        A bike with *both* wheels on?

*Mrs Lyons nods enthusiastically*

**Mrs Lyons**            And he'd sleep every night
                In a bed of his own.
**Mrs Johnstone**        He wouldn't get into fights
                He'd leave matches alone.
                And you'd never find him
                Effin' and blindin'.
                And when he grew up
                He could never be told
                To stand and queue up
                For hours on end at the dole
                He'd grow up to be
**Mrs Lyons**
**Mrs Johnstone** { (*together*) } A credit to me
**Mrs Johnstone**        To you

*Underscoring for the following dialogue*

**Mrs Johnstone** I would still be able to see him every day, wouldn't I?
**Mrs Lyons** Of course.
**Mrs Johnstone** An'.... an' you would look after him, wouldn't y'?
**Mrs Lyons**            I'd keep him warm in the winter
    (*singing*)          And cool when it shines.
                I'd pull out his splinters
                Without making him cry.

I'd always be there
If his dream became a nightmare.

My child.
My child.

*There is a pause before Mrs Johnstone nods. Mrs Lyons goes across and kisses her, hugs her. Mrs Johnstone is slightly embarrassed*

Oh. Now you must help me. There's so much . . . I'll have to . . . (*She takes out the cushion*) We'll do this properly so that it's throughly convincing, and I'll need to see you walk, and baby clothes, I'll have to knit and buy bottles and suffer from piles.

**Mrs Johnstone** What?

**Mrs Lyons** Doesn't one get piles when one's pregnant? And buy a cot and . . . Oh help me with this, Mrs J. Is it in the right place? (*She puts the cushion back again*) I want it to look right before I go shopping.

**Mrs Johnstone** (*helping her with the false pregnancy*) What you goin' the shops for? I do the shopping.

**Mrs Lyons** Oh no, from now on I do the shopping. I want everyone to know about my baby. (*She suddenly reaches for the Bible*)

### Music 7: Underscoring

Mrs J. We must make this a, erm, a binding agreement.

*Mrs Lyons shows the Bible to Mrs Johnstone, who is at first reluctant and then lays her hand on it*

*The Narrator enters. His narration is underscored with a bass note, repeated as a heartbeat*

**Narrator**          In the name of Jesus, the thing was done,
Now there's no going back, for anyone.
It's too late now, for feeling torn
There's a pact been sealed, there's a deal been born.

*Mrs Lyons puts the Bible away. Mrs Johnstone stands and stares as Mrs Lyons grabs shopping bags and takes a last satisfied glance at herself in the mirror*

**Mrs Johnstone** Why . . . why did we have to do that?

**Mrs Lyons** Mrs J, nobody must ever know. Therefore we have to have an agreement.

*Mrs Johnstone nods but is still uncomfortable*

Right, I shan't be long. Bye.

*Mrs Lyons exits*

*Mrs Johnstone stands alone, afraid*

*The heartbeat grows in intensity*

| Narrator | How swiftly those who've made a pact, |
|---|---|
| | Can come to overlook the fact. |
| | Or wish the reckoning be delayed |
| | But a debt is a debt, and must be paid. |

*The Narrator exits*

**Music 8: Underscoring**

*As the heartbeat reaches maximum volume it suddenly stops and is replaced by the sound of crying babies*

*Two nurses appear, each carrying a bundle. A pram is wheeled on*

*The nurses hand the bundles to Mrs Johnstone who places them smiling, into the pram. Making faces and noises at the babies she stops the crying. The babies settled, she sets off, wheeling the pram towards home. The Lights crossfade to the Johnstone home*

*Various debt collectors emerge from her house to confront Mrs Johnstone*

**Catalogue Man** I'm sorry love . . . the kids said you were at the hospital. (*He looks into the pram*) Ah . . . they're lovely, aren't they? I'm sorry love, especially at a time like this, but, you are twelve weeks behind in your payments. I've got to do this, girl . . .

**Finance Man** Y' shouldn't sign for the bloody stuff, missis. If y' know y' can't pay, y' shouldn't bloody well sign.

**Catalogue Man** Look, if y' could give me a couple of weeks' money on this I could leave it.

*Mrs Johnstone shakes her head*

**Finance Man** Y' shouldn't have signed for all this stuff, should y'? Y' knew y' wouldn't be able to pay, didn't y'?

**Mrs Johnstone** (*almost to herself*) When I got me job, I thought I would be able to pay. When I went in the showroom I only meant to come out with a couple of things. But when you're standing there, it all looks so nice. When y' look in the catalogue an' there's six months to pay, it seems years away, an' y' need a few things so y' sign.

**Finance Man** Yeh, well y' bloody well shouldn't.

**Mrs Johnstone** (*coming out of her trance; angrily*) I know I shouldn't, you soft get. I've spent all me bleedin' life knowin' I *shouldn't*. But I do. Now, take y' soddin' wireless an' get off.

**Catalogue Man** Honest love, I'm sorry.

**Mrs Johnstone** It's all right, lad . . . we're used to it. We were in the middle of our tea one night when they arrived for the table. (*She gives a wry laugh*)

**Catalogue Man** Ah well as long as y' can laugh about it, eh, that's the main thing isn't it?

*The Catalogue Man exits*

**Mrs Johnstone** (*not laughing*) Yeh.

### Music 9: Easy Terms

*Other creditors continue to enter the house and leave with goods*

*Mrs Johnstone watches the creditors. The babies begin to cry and she moves to the pram, rocking it gently as she sings, as if to the babies in the pram*

(*Singing*)  Only mine until
The time comes round
To pay the bill.
Then, I'm afraid,
What can't be paid
Must be returned.
You never, ever learn,
That nothing's yours,
On easy terms.

Only for a time,
I must not learn,
To call you mine.
Familiarize
That face, those eyes
Make future plans
That cannot be confirmed.
On borrowed time,
On easy terms.

Living on the never never,
Constant as the changing weather,
Never sure
Who's at the door
Or the price I'll have to pay.

Should we meet again
I will not recognize your name.
You can be sure
What's gone before
Will be concealed.
Your friends will never learn
That once we were
On easy terms.

Living on the never never,
Constant as the changing weather,
Never sure
Who's at the door
Or the price I'll have to pay ...

*Mrs Lyons enters, still with the pregnancy padding*

**Mrs Lyons** They're born, you didn't notify me.

**Mrs Johnstone** Well I ... I just ... it's ... couldn't I keep them for a few more days, please, please, they're a pair, they go together.

**Mrs Lyons** My husband is due back tomorrow, Mrs Johnstone. I must have my baby. We made an agreement, a bargain. You swore on the Bible.

**Mrs Johnstone** You'd better ... you'd better see which one you want.

**Mrs Lyons** I'll take ...

**Mrs Johnstone** No. Don't tell me which one. Just take him, take him.

(*Singing*)            Living on the never never,
                          Constant as the changing weather,
                          Never sure
                          Who's at the door
                          Or the price I'll have to pay,
                          Should we meet again ...

*Mrs Lyons rapidly pulls out the padding from beneath her dress. Amongst it is a shawl which she uses to wrap around the baby before picking it from the pram*

**Mrs Lyons** Thank you Mrs Johnstone, thank you. I'll see you next week.

**Mrs Johnstone** I'm due back tomorrow.

**Mrs Lyons** I know but why don't you ... why don't you take the week off, on full pay of course.

*Mrs Lyons exits*

*Mrs Johnstone turns and enters her house with the remaining twin in the pram*

**Kid One** (*off*) What happened to the other twin, Mother?

**Kid Two** (*off*) Where's the other twinny, Mam?

**Mrs Johnstone** He's gone. He's gone up to heaven, love. He's living with Jesus and the angels.

**Kid Three** (*off*) What's it like there Mam, in heaven?

**Mrs Johnstone** It's lovely son, he'll be well looked after there. He'll have anything he wants.

**Kid One** (*off*) Will he have his own bike?

**Mrs Johnstone** Yeh. With both wheels on.

**Kid One** (*off*) Why can't I have a bike? Eh?

**Mrs Johnstone** I'll ... I'll have a look in the catalogue next week. We'll see what the bikes are like in there.

**Kids** (*together; off*) Mam, I want a Meccano set.
                You said I could have a new dress, Mother.
                Why can't I have an air pistol?
                Let's look in the catalogue now, Mam.
                It's great when we look in the catalogue, Mam.
                Go on, let's all look in the catalogue.

**Mrs Johnstone** I've told y', when I get home, I've got to go to work.

*The Lights crossfade to the Lyons house*

*Mr and Mrs Lyons enter their house and we see them looking at the child in its cot*

*Mrs Johnstone enters and immediately goes about her work*

*Mrs Johnstone stops work for a moment and glances into the cot, beaming and cooing. Mr Lyons is next to her with Mrs Lyons in the background, obviously agitated at Mrs Johnstone's fussing*

Aw, he's really comin' on now, isn't he, Mr Lyons? I'll bet y' dead proud of him, aren't y', aren't y', eh?

**Mr Lyons** (*good naturedly*) Yes . . . yes I am, aren't I, Edward? I'm proud of Jennifer, too.

*Mr Lyons beams at his wife who can hardly raise a smile*

**Mrs Johnstone** Ah . . . he's lovely. (*She coos into the cot*) Ah look, he wants to be picked up, I'll just . . .

**Mrs Lyons** No, no. Mrs Johnstone. He's fine. He doesn't want to be picked up.

**Mrs Johnstone** Ah, but look he's gonna cry . . .

**Mrs Lyons** If he needs picking up, *I* shall pick him up. All right?

**Mrs Johnstone** Well, I just thought, I'm sorry I. . . .

**Mrs Lyons** Yes. Erm, has the bathroom been done? Time is getting on.

**Mrs Johnstone** Oh. Yeh, yeh. . . .

*Mrs Johnstone exits*

**Mr Lyons** Darling. Don't be hard on the woman. She only wanted to hold the baby. All women like to hold babies, don't they?

**Mrs Lyons** I don't want her to hold the baby, Richard. She's . . . I don't want the baby to catch anything. Babies catch things very easily, Richard.

**Mr Lyons** All right, all right, you know best.

**Mrs Lyons** You don't see her as much as I do. She's always fussing over him; any opportunity and she's cooing and cuddling as if she were his mother. She's always bothering him, Richard, always. Since the baby arrived she ignores most of her work. (*She is about to cry*)

**Mr Lyons** Come on, come on . . . It's all right Jennifer. You're just a little . . . it's this depression thing that happens after a woman's had a . . .

**Mrs Lyons** I'm not depressed Richard: it's just that she makes me feel . . . Richard, I think she should go.

**Mr Lyons** And what will you do for help in the house?

**Mrs Lyons** I'll find somebody else. I'll find somebody who doesn't spend all day fussing over the baby.

**Mr Lyons** (*glancing at his watch*) Oh well, I suppose you know best. The house is your domain. Look, Jen, I've got a board meeting. I really must dash.

**Mrs Lyons** Richard, can you let me have some cash?

**Mr Lyons** Of course.

**Mrs Lyons** I need about fifty pounds.

**Mr Lyons** My God, what for?

**Mrs Lyons** I've got lots of things to buy for the baby, I've got the nursery to sort out . . .

**Mr Lyons** All right, all right, here. (*He hands her the money*)

*Mr Lyons exits*

*Mrs Lyons considers what she is about to do and then calls*

**Mrs Lyons** Mrs Johnstone. Mrs Johnstone, would you come out here for a moment, please.

*Mrs Johnstone enters*

**Mrs Johnstone** Yes?

**Mrs Lyons** Sit down. Richard and I have been talking it over and, well the thing is, we both think it would be better if you left.

**Mrs Johnstone** Left where?

**Mrs Lyons** It's your work. Your work has deteriorated.

**Mrs Johnstone** But, I work the way I've always worked.

**Mrs Lyons** Well, I'm sorry, we're not satisfied.

**Mrs Johnstone** What will I do? How are we gonna live without my job?

**Mrs Lyons** Yes, well we've thought of that. Here, here's ... (*She pushes the money into Mrs Johnstone's hands*) It's a lot of money ... but, well ...

**Mrs Johnstone** (*thinking, desperate. Trying to get it together*) OK. All right. All right, Mrs Lyons, right. If I'm goin', I'm takin' my son with me, I'm takin' ...

*As Mrs Johnstone moves towards the cot Mrs Lyons roughly drags her out of the way*

**Mrs Lyons** Oh no, you're not. Edward is my son. Mine.

**Mrs Johnstone** I'll tell someone ... I'll tell the police ... I'll bring the police in an' ...

**Mrs Lyons** No ... no you won't. You gave your baby away. Don't you realize what a crime that is. You'll be locked up. You sold your baby.

*Mrs Johnstone, horrified, sees the bundle of notes in her hand, and throws it across the room*

**Mrs Johnstone** I didn't ... you told me, you said I could see him every day. Well, I'll tell someone, I'm gonna tell ...

*Mrs Johnstone starts to leave but Mrs Lyons stops her*

**Mrs Lyons** No. You'll tell nobody.

### Music 10: Underscoring

Because ... because if you tell anyone ... and these children learn of the truth, then you know what will happen, don't you? You do know what they say about twins, secretly parted, don't you?

**Mrs Johnstone** (*terrified*) What? What?

**Mrs Lyons** They say ... they say that if either twin learns that he was one of a pair, they shall both immediately die. It means, Mrs Johnstone, that these brothers shall grow up, unaware of the other's existence. They shall be raised apart and never, ever told what was once the truth. You won't tell anyone about this, Mrs Johnstone, because if you do, you will kill them.

*Mrs Lyons picks up the money and thrusts it into Mrs Johnstone's hands. Mrs Lyons turns and walks away*

*The Narrator enters*

**Music 11: Shoes Upon The Table (1)**

**Narrator**     Shoes upon the table
An' a spider's been killed.
Someone broke the lookin' glass
A full moon shinin'
An' the salt's been spilled.
You're walkin' on the pavement cracks
Don't know what's gonna come to pass.

Now y' know the devil's got your number,
Y' know he's gonna find y',
Y' know he's right behind y',
He's starin' through your windows
He's creeping down the hall.

Ain't no point in clutching
At your rosary
You're always gonna know what was done
Even when you shut your eyes you still see
That you sold a son
And you can't tell anyone

But y' know the devil's got your number,
Y' know he's gonna find y',
Y' know he's right behind y',
He's starin' through your windows
He's creeping down the hall.

Yes, y' know the devil's got your number
He's gonna find y',
Y' know he's right beyind y',
He's standin' on your step
And he's knocking at your door.
He's knocking at your door,
He's knocking at your door.

*The Narrator exits at the end of the song*

*The Lights crossfade to the Johnstone house*

*During the song Mrs Johnstone has gone to her house and locked herself in*

*Mickey, aged "seven", is knocking incessantly at the door. He is carrying a toy gun*

**Mrs Johnstone** (*screaming; off*) Go away!

**Mickey** Mother ... will y' open the bleedin' door or what?

**Mrs Johnstone** (*realizing; with relief; off*) Mickey?

*Mrs Johnstone comes to open the door*

**Mickey** Mam, Mam.

*She grabs him and hugs him. He extricates himself*

Why was the door bolted? Did you think it was the rent man?

*She laughs and looks at him*

Mam, our Sammy's robbed me other gun an' that was me best one. Why does he rob all me things off me?

**Mrs Johnstone** Because you're the youngest Mickey. It used to happen to our Sammy when he was the youngest.

**Mickey** Mam, we're playin' mounted police an' Indians. I'm a mountie. Mam, Mam, y' know this mornin', we've wiped out three thousand Indians.

**Mrs Johnstone** Good.

**Mickey** (*aiming the gun at her and firing*) Mam, Mam, you're dead.

**Mrs Johnstone** (*staring at him*) Hmm.

**Mickey** What's up, Mam?

**Mrs Johnstone** Nothin' son. Go on, you go out an' play, there's a good lad. But, ey, don't you go playin' with those hooligans down at the rough end.

**Mickey** (*on his way out*) We're down at the other end, near the big houses in the park.

**Mrs Johnstone** Mickey! Come here.

**Mickey** What?

**Mrs Johnstone** What did you say, where have you been playin'?

**Mickey** Mam, I'm sorry, I forgot.

**Mrs Johnstone** What have I told you about playin' up near there. Come here. (*She grabs him*)

**Mickey** It wasn't my fault. Honest.

**Mrs Johnstone** So whose fault was it then?

**Mickey** The Indians. They rode up that way, they were tryin' to escape.

**Mrs Johnstone** Don't you ever go up there. Do you hear me?

**Mickey** Yeh. You let our Sammy go up there.

**Mrs Johnstone** Our Sammy's older than you.

**Mickey** But why ...

**Mrs Johnstone** Just shut up. Never mind why. You don't go up near there. Now go on, get out an' play. But you stay outside the front door where I can see y'.

**Mickey** Ah but, Mam, the ...

**Mrs Johnstone** Go on!

*Mrs Johnstone exits*

*Mickey makes his way outside. He is fed up. Desultory. Shoots down a few imaginary Indians but somehow the magic has gone out of genocide*

*Mickey sits, bored, looking at the ants on the pavement*

**Mickey**          I wish I was our Sammy
  (*reciting*)      Our Sammy's nearly ten.
                    He's got two worms and a catapult
                    An' he's built a underground den.
                    But I'm not allowed to go in there,
                    I have to stay near the gate,
                    'Cos me Mam says I'm only seven,
                    But I'm not, I'm nearly eight!

                    I sometimes hate our Sammy,
                    He robbed me toy car y' know,
                    Now the wheels are missin' an' the top's broke off,
                    An' the bleedin' thing won' go.
                    An' he said when he took it, it was just like that,
                    But it wasn't, it went dead straight,
                    But y' can't say nott'n when they think y' seven
                    An' y' not, y' nearly eight.

                    I wish I was our Sammy,
                    Y' wanna see him spit,
                    Straight in y' eye from twenty yards
                    An' every time a hit.
                    He's allowed to play with matches,
                    And he goes to bed dead late,
                    And I have to go at seven,
                    Even though I'm nearly eight.

                    Y' know our Sammy,
                    He draws nudey women,
                    Without arms, or legs, or even heads
                    In the baths, when he goes swimmin'.
                    But I'm not allowed to go to the baths,
                    Me Mam says I have to wait,
                    'Cos I might get drowned, cos I'm only seven,
                    But I'm not, I'm nearly eight.

                    Y' know our Sammy,
                    Y' know what he sometimes does?
                    He wees straight through the letter box
                    Of the house next door to us.
                    I tried to do it one night,
                    But I had to stand on a crate,
                    'Cos I couldn't reach the letter box
                    But I will by the time I'm eight.

*Bored and petulant, Mickey sits and shoots an imaginary Sammy*

  *Edward, also aged "seven" appears. He is bright and forthcoming*

**Edward**  Hello.

**Mickey** (*suspiciously*) Hello.

**Edward** I've seen you before.

**Mickey** Where?

**Edward** You were playing with some other boys near my house.

**Mickey** Do you live up in the park?

**Edward** Yes. Are you going to come and play up there again?

**Mickey** No. I would do but I'm not allowed.

**Edward** Why?

**Mickey** 'Cos me mam says.

**Edward** Well, my mummy doesn't allow me to play down here actually.

**Mickey** 'Gis a sweet.

**Edward** All right. (*He offers a bag from his pocket*)

**Mickey** (*shocked*) What?

**Edward** Here.

**Mickey** (*trying to work out the catch. Suspiciously taking one*) Can I have another one. For our Sammy?

**Edward** Yes, of course. Take as many as you want.

**Mickey** (*taking a handful*) Are you soft?

**Edward** I don't think so.

**Mickey** Round here if y' ask for a sweet, y' have to ask about, about twenty million times. An' y' know what?

**Edward** (*sitting beside Mickey*) What?

**Mickey** They still don't bleedin' give y' one. Sometimes our Sammy does but y' have to be dead careful if our Sammy gives y' a sweet.

**Edward** Why?

**Mickey** Cos, if our Sammy gives y' a sweet he's usually weed on it first.

**Edward** (*exploding in giggles*) Oh, that sounds like super fun.

**Mickey** It is. If y' our Sammy.

**Edward** Do you want to come and play?

**Mickey** I might do. But I'm not playin' now cos I'm pissed off.

**Edward** (*awed*) Pissed off. You say smashing things don't you? Do you know any more words like that?

**Mickey** Yeh. Yeh, I know loads of words like that. Y' know, like the "F" word.

**Edward** (*clueless*) Pardon?

**Mickey** The "F" word.

*Edward is still puzzled. Mickey looks round to check that he cannot be overheard, then whispers the word to Edward. The two of them immediately wriggle and giggle with glee*

**Edward** What does it mean?

**Mickey** I don't know. It sounds good though, doesn't it?

**Edward** Fantastic. When I get home I'll look it up in the dictionary.

**Mickey** In the what?

**Edward** The dictionary. Don't you know what a dictionary is?

**Mickey** 'Course I do. . . . It's a, it's a thingy innit?

**Edward** A book which explains the meaning of words. . . .

**Mickey** The meaning of words, yeh. Our Sammy'll be here soon. I hope he's in a good mood. He's dead mean sometimes.

**Edward** Why?

**Mickey** It's cos he's got a plate in his head.

**Edward** A plate. In his head?

**Mickey** Yeh. When he was little, me Mam was at work an' our Donna Marie was supposed to be lookin' after him but he feel out the window an' broke his head. So they took him to the hospital an' put a plate in his head.

**Edward** A plate. A dinner plate?

**Mickey** I don't think so, cos our Sammy's head's not really that big. I think it must have been one of them little plates that you have bread off.

**Edward** A side plate?

**Mickey** No, it's on the top.

**Edward** And . . . and can you see the shape of it, in his head.

**Mickey** I suppose, I suppose if y' looked under his hair.

**Edward** (*after a reflective pause*) You know the most smashing things. Will you be my best friend?

**Mickey** Yeh. If y' want.

**Edward** What's your name?

**Mickey** Michael Johnstone. But everyone calls me Mickey. What's yours?

**Edward** Edward Lyons.

**Mickey** D' they call y' Eddie?

**Edward** No.

**Mickey** Well, I will.

**Edward** Will you?

**Mickey** Yeh. How old are y' Eddie?

**Edward** Seven.

**Mickey** I'm older than you. I'm nearly eight.

**Edward** Well, I'm nearly eight, really.

**Mickey** What's your birthday?

**Edward** July the eighteenth.

**Mickey** So is mine.

**Edward** Is it really?

**Mickey** Ey, we were born on the same day . . . that means we can be blood brothers. Do you wanna be my blood brother, Eddie?

**Edward** Yes, please.

**Mickey** (*producing a penknife*) It hurts y' know. (*He puts a nick in his hand*) Now, give us yours.

*Mickey nicks Edward's hand, then they clamp hands together*

See this means that we're blood brothers, an' that we always have to stand by each other. Now you say after me: "I will always defend my brother".

**Edward** I will always defend my brother . . .

**Mickey** And stand by him.

**Edward** And stand by him.

**Mickey** An' share all my sweets with him.

**Edward** And share . . .

*Sammy leaps in front of them, gun in hand, pointed at them*

**Mickey** Hi ya, Sammy.
**Sammy** Give us a sweet.
**Mickey** Haven't got any.
**Edward** Yes, you have ...

*Mickey frantically shakes his head, trying to shut Edward up*

Yes, I gave you one for Sammy, remember?

*Sammy laughs at Edward's voice and Mickey's misfortune*

**Sammy** Y' little robbin' get.
**Mickey** No, I'm not. (*He hands over a sweet*) An' anyway, you pinched my best gun.

*Mickey tries to snatch the gun from Sammy, but Sammy is too fast*

**Sammy** It's last anyway. It only fires caps. I'm gonna get a real gun soon, I'm gonna get an air gun.

*Sammy goes into a fantasy shoot out. He doesn't notice Edward who has approached him and is craning to get a close look at his head*

(*Eventually noticing*) What are you lookin' at?
**Edward** Pardon.
**Mickey** That's Eddie. He lives up by the park.
**Sammy** He's a friggin' poshy.
**Mickey** No, he's not. He's my best friend.
**Sammy** (*snorting, deciding it's not worth the bother*) You're soft. Y' just soft little kids. (*In quiet disdain he moves away*)
**Mickey** Where y' goin'?
**Sammy** (*looking at Mickey*) I've gonna do another burial. Me worms have died again.
**Mickey** (*excitedly; to Edward*) Oh, y' comin' the funeral? Our Sammy is havin' a funeral. Can we come, Sammy?

*Sammy puts his hand into his pocket and brings forth a handful of soil*

**Sammy** Look, they was alive an wrigglin' this mornin'. But by dinner time they was dead.

*Mickey and Edward inspect the deceased worms in Sammy's hand*

*Mrs Johnstone enters*

**Mrs Johnstone** Mickey ... Mickey ...
**Edward** Is that your mummy?
**Mickey** Mam ... Mam, this is my brother.
**Mrs Johnstone** (*stunned*) What?
**Mickey** My blood brother, Eddie.
**Mrs Johnstone** Eddie, Eddie who?
**Edward** Edward Lyons, Mrs Johnstone.

*Mrs Johnstone stands still, staring at him*

**Mickey** Eddie's my best friend, Mam. He lives up by the park an' ...
**Mrs Johnstone** Mickey ... get in the house.
**Mickey** What?
**Mrs Johnstone** Sammy, you an' all. Both of y' get in.
**Sammy** But I'm older than him, I don't have to ...
**Mrs Johnstone** I said get, the pair of y' ...
**Mickey** (*going, almost in tears*) But I haven't done nothin'. I'll see y' Eddie.
Ta ra, Eddie ...

*Mickie exits into the house*

**Mrs Johnstone** Sammy!
**Sammy** Ah. (*To Edward*) I'll get you.
**Edward** Have I done something wrong, Mrs Johnstone?
**Mrs Johnstone** Does your mother know that you're down here?

*Edward shakes his head*

An' what would she say if she did know?
**Edward** I ... I think she'd be angry?
**Mrs Johnstone** So don't you think you better get home before she finds out?
**Edward** Yes.
**Mrs Johnstone** Go on, then.

*Edward turns to go, then stops*

**Edward** Could I ... would it be all right if I came to play with Mickey on
another day? Or perhaps he could come to play at my house ...
**Mrs Johnstone** Don't you ever come round here again. Ever.
**Edward** But ...
**Mrs Johnstone** Ever! Now go on. Beat it, go home before the bogey man
gets y'.

*Edward walks towards his home. As he goes Mrs Johnstone reprises "Easy
Terms". The Lights crossfade to the Lyons' house*

### Music 12: Easy Terms (reprise)

Should we meet again,
I will not recognize your name,
You can be sure
What's gone before
Will be concealed.
Your friends will never learn
That once we were
On easy terms.

*Mr and Mrs Lyons enter their house as Edward walks home*

*Edward reaches his home and walks in. His mother hugs him and his father
produces a toy gun for him. Edward, delighted, seizes it and "shoots" his
father, who spiritedly "dies" to Edward's great amusement. Edward and his
father romp on the floor. Mrs Lyons settles herself in an armchair with a story*

*book, calling Edward over to her. Edward goes and sits with her, Mr Lyons joining them and sitting on the arm of the chair*

*Mrs Johnstone turns and goes into her house at the end of the song*

*Mr Lyons gets up and walks towards the door*

**Edward** Daddy ... we haven't finished the story yet.
**Mr Lyons** Mummy will read the story, Edward. I've got to go to work for an hour.

*Mrs Lyons gets up and goes to her husband, Edward goes to the bookshelf and leafs through a dictionary*

**Mrs Lyons** Richard you didn't say ...
**Mr Lyons** Darling, I'm sorry, but if, if we complete this merger I will, I promise you, have more time. That's why we're doing it, Jen. If we complete this, the firm will run itself and I'll have plenty of time to spend with you both.
**Mrs Lyons** I just—it's not me, it's Edward. You should spend more time with him. I don't want—I don't want him growing away from you.
**Edward** Daddy, how do you spell bogey man?
**Mr Lyons** Ask Mummy. Darling, I'll see you later now. Must dash.

*Mr Lyons exits*

**Edward** Mummy, how do you spell bogey man?
**Mrs Lyons** Mm?
**Edward** Bogey man?
**Mrs Lyons** (*laughing*) Edward, wherever did you hear such a thing?
**Edward** I'm trying to look it up.
**Mrs Lyons** There's no such thing as a bogey man. It's a—a superstition. The sort of thing a silly mother might say to her children—"the bogey man will get you".
**Edward** Will he get me?
**Mrs Lyons** Edward, I've told you, there's no such thing.

*A doorbell is heard (see Vocal Score)*

*Mrs Lyons goes to answer the door*

**Mickey** (*off*) Does Eddie live here?
**Mrs Lyons** (*off*) Pardon?
**Mickey** (*off*) Does he? Is he comin' out to play, eh?
**Edward** (*shouting*) Mickey!

*Mickey enters, pursued by Mrs Lyons*

**Mickey** Hi-ya, Eddie. I've got our Sammy's catapult. Y' comin' out?
**Edward** Oh! (*He takes the catapult and trys a practice shot*) Isn't Mickey fantastic, Mum?
**Mrs Lyons** Do you go to the same school as Edward?
**Mickey** No.

**Edward** Mickey says smashing things. We're blood brothers, aren't we, Mickey?

**Mickey** Yeh. We were born on the same day.

**Edward** Come on Mickey, let's go . . .

**Mrs Lyons** Edward . . . Edward, it's time for bed.

**Edward** Mummy. It's not.

*Mrs Lyons, takes over and ushers Mickey out*

**Mrs Lyons** I'm very sorry, but it's Edward's bedtime.

**Edward** Mummy. Mummy it's early.

*Mrs Lyons exits with Mickey to show him out. Then she returns*

Mummy!

**Mrs Lyons** Edward. Edward where did you meet that boy?

**Edward** At his house.

**Mrs Lyons** And . . . and his second name is Johnstone, isn't it?

**Edward** Yes. And I think you're very, very mean.

**Mrs Lyons** I've told you never to go where that boy—where boys like that live.

**Edward** But why?

**Mrs Lyons** Because, because you're not the same as him. You're not, do you understand?

**Edward** No, I don't understand. And I hate you!

**Mrs Lyons** (*almost crying*) Edward, Edward, don't. It's . . . what I'm doing is only for your own good. It's only because I love you, Edward.

**Edward** You don't you don't. If you loved me you'd let me go out with Mickey because he's my best friend. I like him more than you.

**Mrs Lyons** Edward. Edward don't say that. Don't ever say that.

**Edward** Well. Well it's true. And I will say it. I know what you are.

**Mrs Lyons** What? What!

**Edward** You're . . . you're a fuckoff!

*Mrs Lyons hits Edward hard and instinctively*

**Mrs Lyons** You see, you see why I don't want you mixing with boys like that! You learn filth from them and behave like this like a, like a horrible little boy, like them. But you are not like them. You are my son, mine, and you won't, you won't ever . . .

*She notices the terror in Edward's face and realizes how heavy she has been. Gently she pulls him to her and cradles him*

Oh, my son . . . my beautiful, beautiful son.

*The Lights crossfade to the street*

*The scene fades as the next scene begins. We hear cap guns and the sound of children making Indian whoops*

*The children rush on playing cowboys and Indians; cops and robbers; goodies and baddies etc.*

*During the huge battle Mrs Lyons exits*

*Edward remains on stage, in the background, as though in his garden, watching, unnoticed by the battling children. Mickey and Linda are in one gang, Sammy in another. The general shoot-out is finally focused on Sammy and Linda*

**Sammy** (*singing acapella, kids' rhyme*)
                I got y'
                I shot y'
                An' y' bloody know I did
                I got y'
                I shot y'
**Linda**         .     I stopped it with the bin lid

*There is a mass of derisive jeers from the other side*

### Music 13: Kids Game

(*Singing*)      But you know that if you cross your fingers
                And if you count from one to ten
                You can get up off the ground again
                It doesn't matter
                The whole thing's just a game

*The shooting starts all over again. A Kid raps on the door of a house. Linda, as a "Moll" appears*

**Kid**             My name is Elliot Ness,
                And lady, here's my card,
                I'm lookin' for one Al Capone
(*To Lackeys*)    Mac, check the back,
                Sarge, you check the yard!
**Linda**           But pal, I've told y'
                Al ain't home.

*We see "Al" make a break for it. Ness shoots him like he was eatin' his breakfast*

**Kid**             So, lady can I use your telephone.

*As Ness goes to the phone and orders a hearse we see Al get up and sing the chorus with the other children*

                But you know that if you cross your fingers,
                And if you count from one to ten,
                You can get up off the ground again,
                It doesn't matter the whole thing's just a game.

*The Kid who was playing Al becomes a cowboy. He turns to face Sammy and sings*

**Cowboy**        When I say draw,
                You'd better grab that gun,

An' maybe say a littler prayer
Cos I'm the fastest draw
That man you ever saw.
Call up your woman, say goodbye to her,
Cos y' know you're goin' right down there.

*As he draws his gun on Sammy, Sammy produces a bazooka and blows him off the stage*

**All**              But you know that if you cross your fingers,
And if you count from one to ten,
You can get up off the ground again,
It doesn't matter,
The whole thing's just a game.

*A group of children become a brigade of US troops*

**Sergeant**      OK men, let's get them
With a hand grenade.
**Corporal**      Let's see them try and get outta this.
**Rest**           He's a hot shot Sergeant
From the Ninth Brigade
He's never been known to miss
**Sergeant**      C'mon give Daddy a kiss.
   *(to grenade)*    *(He pulls the pin and lobs it)*

*His brigade cover their ears and crouch, down. Linda catches the grenade and lobs it back at them. After being blown to pieces they get up singing the chorus, along with the "enemy"*

**All**              But you know that if you cross your fingers,
And if you count from one to ten.
You can get up off the ground again,
It doesn't matter,
The whole thing's just a game.

*Sammy comes forward as Professor Howe carrying a condom filled with water*

**Professor**      My name's Professor Howe,
An' zees bomb I 'old,
Eet can destroy ze 'emisphere,
I've primed it, I've timed it
To explode,
Unless you let me out of here (NO?)

*They don't*

Then I suggest you cover your ears

*There is an explosion which tops them all. Out of it come all the children singing the chorus*

**All**              But you know that if you cross your fingers,
And if you count from one to ten,

> You can get up off the ground again,
> It doesn't matter,
> The whole thing's just a game
> The whole thing's just a game
> The whole thing's just a . . .

**Sammy** (*interrupting; chanting*)
> You're dead
> Y' know y' are
> I got y' standin'
> Near that car

**Linda**
> But when y' did
> His hand was hid
> Behind his back
> His fingers crossed
> An' so he's not

**Mickey**
> So you fuck off!

*All the children, apart from Mickey and Linda, point and chant the accusing "Aah!" Mickey is singled out, accused. The rest, led by Sammy suddenly chant at Mickey and point*

**All**
(*chanting*)
> You said the "F" word
> You're gonna die
> You'll go to hell an' there you'll fry
> Just like a fish in a chip shop fat
> Only twenty five million times hotter than that!

*They all laugh at Mickey*

*Linda moves in to protect Mickey who is visibly shaken*

**Linda** Well, well, all youse lot swear, so you'll all go to hell with him.
**Sammy** No, we won't Linda.
**Linda** Why?
**Sammy** 'Cos when we swear . . . we cross our fingers!
**Mickey** Well, my fingers were crossed.
**Children**        No they weren't.
(*variously*)      Liar!
                         Come off it.
                         I seen them.
**Linda** Leave him alone!
**Sammy** Why? What'll you do about it if we don't?
**Linda** (*undaunted; approaching Sammy*) I'll tell my mother why all her ciggies always disappear when you're in our house.
**Sammy** What?
**Linda** An' the half crowns.
**Sammy** (*suddenly*) Come on gang, let's go. We don't wanna play with these anyway. They're just kids.

*The other children fire a barrage of "shots" at Mickey and Linda before they rush off*

**Linda** I hate them!

*Linda notices Mickey quietly crying*

What's up?

**Mickey** I don't wanna die.

**Linda** But y' have to Mickey. Everyone does. (*She starts to dry his tears*) Like your twinny died, didn't he, when he was a baby. See, look on the bright side of it, Mickey. When you die you'll meet your twinny again, won't y'?

**Mickey** Yeh.

**Linda** An' listen Mickey, if y' dead, there's no school, is there?

**Mickey** (*smiling*) An' I don't care about our Sammy, anyway. Look. (*He produces an air pistol*) He thinks no one knows he's got it. But I know where he hides it.

**Linda** (*impressed*) Ooh ... gis a go.

**Mickey** No ... come on, let's go get Eddie first.

**Linda** Who?

**Mickey** Come on, I'll show y'.

*They go as if to Edward's garden*

**Mickey** (*loud but conspiratorially*) Eddie ... Eddie ... y' comin' out?

**Edward** I ... My mum says I haven't got to play with you.

**Mickey** Well, my mum says I haven't got to play with you. But take no notice of mothers. They're soft. Come on, I've got Linda with me. She's a girl but she's all right.

*Edward decides to risk it and creeps out*

**Mickey** Hi-ya.

**Edward** Hi-ya, Mickey. Hello, Linda.

**Linda** Hi-ya, Eddie. (*She produces the air pistol*) Look ... we've got Sammy's air gun.

**Mickey** Come on, Eddie. You can have a shot at our target in the park.

**Linda** Peter Pan.

**Mickey** We always shoot at that, don't we, Linda?

**Linda** Yeh, we try an' shoot his little thingy off, don't we, Mickey?

*They all laugh*

Come on gang, let's go.

**Edward** (*standing firm*) But Mickey ... I mean ... suppose we get caught ... by a policeman.

**Mickey** Aah ... take no notice. We've been caught loads of times by a policeman ... haven't we, Linda?

**Linda** Oh, my God, yeh. Hundreds of times. More than that.

**Mickey** We say dead funny things to them, don't we, Linda?

**Edward** What sort of funny things?

**Linda** All sorts, don't we Mickey?

**Mickey** Yeh ... like y' know when they ask what y' name is, we say things like, like "Adolph Hitler", don't we, Linda?

**Linda** Yeh, an' hey Eddie, y' know when they say, "What d' y' think you're doin'"? we always say somethin' like like, "waitin' for the ninety-two bus".

*Mickey and Linda crease up with laughter*

Come on.

**Edward** (*greatly impressed*) Do you ... do you really? Goodness, that's fantastic.

**Mickey** Come on, bunk under y' fence, y' Ma won't see y'.

*Mickey, Linda and Edward exit*

*Mrs Lyons enters the garden*

**Mrs Lyons** (*calling*) Edward, Edward, Edward ...

*The Narrator enters*

### Music 15: Shoes Upon the Table (reprise—2a)

**Narrator**     There's gypsies in the wood,
(*singing*)      An' they've been watchin' you,
                 They're gonna take your baby away.
                 There's gypsies in the wood,
                 An' they've been calling you,
                 Can Edward please come out and play,
                 Please can he come with us and play.

                 You know the devil's got your number,
                 Y' know he's gonna find y',
                 Y' know he's right behind y',
                 He's staring through your windows,
                 He's creeping down the hall.

*Mr Lyons enters the garden*

**Mrs Lyons** Oh Richard, Richard.

**Mr Lyons** For God's sake Jennifer, I told you on the phone, he'll just be out playing somewhere.

**Mrs Lyons** But where?

**Mr Lyons** Outside somewhere, with friends. Edward ...

**Mrs Lyons** But I don't want him out playing.

**Mr Lyons** Jennifer, he's not a baby. Edward ...

**Mrs Lyons** I don't care, I don't care ...

**Mr Lyons** For Christ's sake, you bring me home from work in the middle of the day, just to say you haven't seen him for an hour. Perhaps we should be talking about you getting something for your nerves.

**Mrs Lyons** There's nothing wrong with my nerves. It's just ... just this place ... I hate it. Richard, I don't want to stay here any more. I want to move.

**Mr Lyons** Jennifer! Jennifer, how many times ... the factory is here, my work is here ...

**Mrs Lyons** It doesn't have to be somewhere far away. But we have got to move, Richard. Becuase if we stay here I feel that something terrible will happen, something bad.

*Mr Lyons sighs and puts his arm round Mrs Lyons*

**Mr Lyons** Look, Jen. What is this thing you keep talking about getting away from? Mm?
**Mrs Lyons** It's just ... it's these people ... these people that Edward has started mixing with. Can't you see how he's drawn to them? They're ... they're drawing him away from me.

*Mr Lyons, in despair, turns away from her*

**Mr Lyons** Oh, Christ.

*He turns to look at her but she looks away. He sighs and absently bends to pick up a pair of child's shoes from the floor*

I do really think you should see a doctor.
**Mr Lyons** (*snapping*) I don't need to see a doctor. I just need to move away from this neighbourhood, because I'm frightened. I'm frightened for Edward.

*Mr Lyons places the shoes on the table before turning on her*

**Mr Lyons** Frightened of what, woman?
**Mrs Lyons** (*wheeling to face him*) Frightened of ... (*She is stopped by the sight of the shoes on the table. She rushes at the table and sweep the shoes off*)

*The Lights fade to a single spot on Mrs Lyons*

### Music 16: Shoes Upon The Table (reprise—2b)

**Narrator**      There's shoes upon the table
(*singing*)       An' a spider's been killed
                  Someone broke the lookin' glass
                  There's a full moon shinin'
                  An' the salt's been spilled
                  You're walkin' on pavement cracks
                  Don't know what's gonna come to pass

                  Now you know the devil's got your number
                  He's gonna find y'
                  Y' know he's right beyind y'
                  He's starin' through your windows
                  He's creeping down the hall.

*The song ends with a percussive build to a sudden full stop and the scene snaps from Mrs Lyons to the children*

*Mickey, Eddie and Linda are standing in line, taking it in turns to fire the air pistol. Mickey takes aim and fires*

**Linda** (*with glee*) Missed.

*Edward loads and fires*

Missed!

*Linda takes the gun and fires. We hear a metallic ping. She beams a satisfied smile at Mickey who ignores it and reloads, fires. The routine is repeated with exactly the same outcome until*

**Mickey** (*taking the gun*) We're not playin' with the gun no more. (*He puts it away*)

**Linda** Ah, why?

**Mickey** It gets broke if y' use it too much.

**Edward** What are we going to do now, Mickey?

**Mickey** I dunno.

**Linda** I do.

**Mickey** What?

**Linda** Let's throw some stones through them windows.

**Mickey** (*brightening*) Ooh, I dare y' Linda, I dare y'.

**Linda** (*picking up a stone*) I will.

**Mickey** (*bending for a stone*) Well, I will. I'm not scared, either. Are you Eddie?

**Edward** Erm ... well ... erm ...

**Linda** He is look. Eddie's scared.

**Mickey** No, he isn't! Are y', Eddie?

**Edward** (*stoically*) No ... I'm not. I'm not scared at all, actually.

**Linda** Right, when I count to three we all throw together. One, two, three ...

*Unseen by them a Policeman has approached behind them*

**Policeman** Me mother caught a flea, she put it in the tea pot to make a cup of tea. ... And what do you think you're doing?

*Linda and Mickey shoot terrified glances at Eddie, almost wetting themselves*

**Edward** (*mistaking their look for encouragement*) Waiting for the ninety-two bus. (*He explodes with excited laughter*)

**Linda** He's not with us.

**Mickey** Sir.

**Linda** Sir.

**Policeman** No. He's definitely with us. What's your name, son?

**Edward** Adolph Hitler.

*Edward laughs until through the laughter he senses that all is not well. He sees that he alone is laughing. The laughter turns to tears which sets the other two off*

*The three children turn round, crying, bawling, followed by the Policeman*

*The three children exit*

*The Lights crossfade to the Johnstone house*

*Mrs Johnstone enters*

*The Policeman goes to confront Mrs Johnstone*

**Policeman** And he was about to commit a serious crime, love. Now, do you understand that? You don't wanna end up in court again, do y'?

*Mrs Johnstone shakes her head*

Well, that's what's gonna happen if I have any more trouble from one of yours. I warned you last time, didn't I, Mrs Johnstone, about your Sammy?

*Mrs Johnstone nods*

Well, there'll be no more bloody warnings from now on. Either you keep them in order, Missis, or it'll be the courts for you, or worse, won't it?

*Mrs Johnstone nods*

Yes, it will.

*As the Policeman turns and goes towards the Lyons house the introduction for Music 17 is heard*

**Music 17: Bright New Day** (preview)

**Mrs Johnstone**    Maybe some day
We'll move away
And start all over again
In some new place
Where they don't know my face
And nobody's heard of my name
Where we can begin again
Feel we can win an' then ...
Maybe ...

*The Lights crossfade to the Lyons house*

*The music tails off as we see the Policeman confronting Mr Lyons. The Policeman has removed his helmet and holds a glass of scotch. Edward is there*

**Policeman** An er, as I say, it was more of a prank, really, Mr Lyons. I'd just dock his pocket money if I was you. (*Laughs*) But, one thing I would say, if y'don't mind me sayin', is well, I'm not sure I'd let him mix with the likes of them in future. Make sure he keeps with his own kind, Mr Lyons. Well er, thanks for the drink, sir. All the best now. He's a good lad, aren't you Adolph? Goodnight, sir. (*He replaces his helmet*)

*The Policeman leaves*

**Mr Lyons** Edward ... how would you like to move to another house?
**Edward** Why, Daddy?
**Mr Lyons** Erm, well, various reasons really. Erm, actually Mummy's not been too well lately and we thought a move, perhaps further out towards the country somewhere, might ... Do you think you'd like that?

**Edward** I want to stay here.
**Mr Lyons** Well, you think about it, old chap.

*Edward leaves his home and goes to the Johnstone's door. He knocks at the door*

*Mrs Johnstone answers the door*

**Edward** Hello, Mrs Johnstone. How are you?
**Mrs Johnstone** You what?
**Edward** I'm sorry. Is there something wrong?
**Mrs Johnstone** No, I just ... I don't usually have kids enquiring about my health. I'm er ... I'm all right. An' how are you, Master Lyons?
**Edward** Very well, thank you.

*Mrs Johnstone looks at Edward for a moment*

**Mrs Johnstone** Yeh. You look it. Y' look very well. Does your mother look after you?
**Edward** Of course.
**Mrs Johnstone** Now listen, Eddie, I told you not to come around here again.
**Edward** I'm sorry but I just wanted to see Mickey.
**Mrs Johnstone** No. It's best ... if ...
**Edward** I won't be coming here again. Ever. We're moving away. To the country.
**Mrs Johnstone** Lucky you.
**Edward** But I'd much rather live here.
**Mrs Johnstone** Would you? When are y' goin'?
**Edward** Tomorrow.
**Mrs Johnstone** Oh. So we really won't see you again, eh ...

*Edward shakes his head and begins to cry*

What's up?
**Edward** (*through his tears*) I don't want to go. I want to stay here where my friends are ... where Mickey is.
**Mrs Johnstone** Come here.

*She takes him, cradling him, letting him cry*

Now listen ... listen, don't you be soft. You'll probably love it in your new house. You'll meet lots of new friends an' in no time at all you'll forget Mickey ever existed.
**Edward** I won't ... I won't. I'll never forget.
**Mrs Johnstone** Shush, shush. Listen, listen Eddie, here's you wantin' to stay here, an' here's me, I've been tryin' to get out for years. We're a right pair, aren't we, you an' me?
**Edward** Why don't you Mrs Johnstone? Why don't you buy a new house near us?
**Mrs Johnstone** Just like that?
**Edward** Yes, yes.

**Mrs Johnstone** Ey.

**Edward** Yes.

**Mrs Johnstone** Would you like a picture of Mickey, to take with you? So's you could remember him?

**Edward** Yes, please.

*She removes a locket from around her neck*

**Mrs Johnstone** See, look ... there's Mickey, there. He was just a young kid when that was taken.

**Edward** And is that you Mrs Johnstone?

*She nods*

Can I really have this?

**Mrs Johnstone** Yeh. But keep it a secret eh, Eddie? Just our secret, between you an' me.

**Edward** (*smiling*) All right, Mrs Johnstone. (*He puts the locket round his neck*)

*He looks at her a moment too long*

**Mrs Johnstone** What y' lookin' at?

**Edward** I thought you didn't like me. I thought you weren't very nice. But I think you're smashing.

**Mrs Johnstone** (*looking at him*) God help the girls when you start dancing.

**Edward** Pardon.

**Mrs Johnstone** Nothing. (*Calling into the house*) Mickey, say goodbye to Eddie—he's moving.

*Mickey comes out of the house*

*The underscoring for Music 18 is quietly introduced*

*Eddie moves to Mickey and gives him a small parcel from his pocket. Mickey unwraps a toy gun. The two boys clasp hands and wave goodbye. Mrs Johnstone and Mickey watch as Edward joins his parents, dressed in outdoor clothes, on their side of the stage*

**Edward** Goodbye.

**Mr Lyons** Well, Edward ... do you like it here?

**Edward** (*unenthusiastically*) It's very nice.

**Mrs Lyons** Oh, look, Edward ... look at those trees and those cows. Oh Edward you're going to like it so much out here, aren't you?

**Edward** Yes. Are you feeling better now, Mummy?

**Mrs Lyons** Much better now, darling. Oh Edward, look, look at those birds ... Look at that lovely black and white one ...

**Edward** (*immediately covering his eyes*) Don't Mummy, don't look. It's a magpie, never look at one magpie. It's one for sorrow ...

**Mr Lyons** Edward ... that's just stupid superstition.

**Edward** It's not, Mickey told me.

**Mrs Lyons** Edward, I think we can forget the silly things that Mickey said.

**Edward** I'm going inside. I want to read.

*Edward exits*

**Mr Lyons** (*comforting his wife*) Children take time to adapt to new surroundings. He'll be as right as rain in a few days. He won't even remember he once lived somewhere else.

*Mrs Lyons forces a smile and allows herself to be led inside by her husband*

*The introduction to Music 18 underscores as we see Mickey ring the doorbell (see Vocal Score) of Edward's old house*

*A Woman answers the door*

**Woman** Yes?
**Mickey** Is er . . . is Eddie in?
**Woman** Eddie? I'm afraid Eddie doesn't live here now.
**Mickey** Oh, yeh. (*He stands looking at the woman*)
**Woman** Goodbye.
**Mickey** Do y' . . . erm, do y' know where he lives now?
**Woman** Pardon?
**Mickey** See, I've got some money, I was gonna go, on the bus, an' see him. Where does he live now?
**Woman** I'm afraid I've no idea.
**Mickey** It's somewhere in the country, isn't it?
**Woman** Look, I honestly don't know and I'm rather busy. Goodbye.

*The Woman closes the door on Mickey*

*Mickey wanders away, aimless and bored, deserted and alone*

### Music 18: Long Sunday Afternoon

**Mickey**         No kids out on the street today,
(*singing*)         You could be living on the moon.
              Maybe everybody's packed their bags and moved away,
              Gonna be a long, long, long,
              Sunday Afternoon

              Just killing time and kicking cans around,
              Try to remember jokes I knew,
              I tell them to myself, but they're not funny since I found
              It's gonna be a long, long, long,
              Sunday Afternoon

*We see Edward, in his garden, equally bored and alone. The scene appears in such a way that we don't know if it is real or in Mickey's mind*

              My best friend
              Always had sweets to share, (He)
              Knew every word in the dictionary.
              He was clean, neat and tidy,
              From Monday to Friday,
              I wish that I could be like,
              Wear clean clothes, talk properly like,
              Do sums and history like,

**Edward** ⎫ (*together*) ⎰ My friend
**Mickey** ⎭            ⎱ My friend
**Edward**              My best freind
                       He could swear like a soldier
                       You would laugh till you died
                       At the stories he told y'
                       He was untidy
                       From Monday to Friday
                       I wish that I could be like
                       Kick a ball and climb a tree like
                       Run around with dirty knees like

**Edward** ⎫ (*together*) ⎰ My friend
**Mickey** ⎭            ⎱ My friend

*The Lights fade on Edward as the music shifts back to "Long Sunday Afternoon"*

**Mickey**             Feels like everybody stayed in bed
                       Or maybe I woke up too soon.
                       Am I the last survivor
                       Is everybody dead?
                       On this long long long
                       Sunday Afternoon

*The Lights crossfade to the Johnstone house*

*Mrs Johnstone appears, clutching a letter*

### Music 19: Bright New Day (reprise)

**Mrs Johnstone**      Oh, bright new day,
   (*singing*)         We're movin' away.
**Mickey** (*speaking*) Mam? What's up?
**Mrs Johnstone** (*singing*) We're startin' all over again.

*Donna Marie enters together with various neighbours*

**Donna Marie** (*speaking*) Is it a summons, Mother?
**Mrs Johnstone**      Oh, bright new day,
   (*singing*)         We're goin' away.
**Mickey** (*calling*) Sammy!

*Mrs Johnstone addresses the various onlookers*

**Mrs Johnstone** (*singing*) Where nobody's heard of our name.

*Sammy enters*

**Sammy** (*speaking*) I never robbed nothin', honest, mam.
**Mrs Johnstone**      Where we can begin again,
   (*singing*)         Feel we can win and then
                       Live just like livin' should be.
                       Got a new situation,

|                         | A new destination, |
|-------------------------|--------------------|
|                         | And no reputation following me |
| **Mickey** (*speaking*) | What is it, what is it? |
| **Mrs Johnstone**       | We're gettin' out, |
| (*singing*)             | We're movin' house, |
|                         | We're starting all over again. |
|                         | We're leavin' this mess |
|                         | For our new address (*pointing it out*) |
|                         | "Sixty five Skelmersdale Lane" |
| **Mickey** (*speaking; worried*) | Where's that, mam? |
| **Sammy** (*speaking*)  | Is that in the country? |
| **Donna Marie** (*speaking*) | What's it like there? |
| **Mrs Johnstone**       | The air is so pure, |
| (*singing*)             | You get drunk just by breathing, |
|                         | And the washing stays clean on the line. |
|                         | Where there's space for the kids, |
|                         | 'Cos the garden's so big, |
|                         | It would take you a week just to reach the far side |

(*Speaking*) Come on, Sammy, Mickey, now you've all gorra help. (*To the neighbours, in a "posh" voice*) Erm would youse excuse us, we've gorra pack. We're movin' away.

*Mrs Johnstone and the children go in to pack*

| **Neighbour** | What did she say? |
|---------------|-------------------|
| **Milkman**   | They're movin away. |
| **All**       | Praise the Lord, he has delivered us at last. |
| **Neighbour** | They're gettin out, |
|               | They're movin' house, |
|               | Life won't be the same as in the past. |
| **Policeman** | I can safely predict |
|               | A sharp drop in the crime rate. |
| **Neighbour** | It'll be calm an' peaceful around here. |
| **Milkman**   | AND now I might even |
|               | Get paid what is mine, mate. |
| **Neighbour** | An' you'll see, grafitti will soon disappear |

*Mrs Johnstone marches out of the house carrying battered suitcases, followed by the children who are struggling to get out some of the items mentioned in the verse*

| **Mrs Johnstone** | Just pack up the bags, |
|-------------------|------------------------|
|                   | We're leavin' the rags, |
|                   | The wobbly wardrobe, chest of drawers that never close. |
|                   | The two legged chair, the carpet so bare, |
|                   | You wouldn't see it if it wasn't for the holes. |
|                   | Now that we're movin' |
|                   | Now that we're improvin', |
|                   | Let's just wash our hands of this lot. |

For it's no longer fitting, for me to be sitting
On a sofa, I know for a fact, was knocked off.

*Her last line is delivered to Sammy who indicates the Policeman, trying to get
her to shut up*

We might get a car,
Be all "lardie dah",
An' go drivin' out to the sands.
At the weekend,
A gentleman friend,
Might take me dancing
To the local bands.
We'll have a front room,
And then if it shoold happen,
That His Holiness flies in from Rome,
He can sit there with me, eating toast, drinking tea
In the sort of surroundings that remind him of home.

**Mickey** (*speaking*) It's like the country, isn't it, mam?

**Mrs Johnstone** (*speaking*) Ey, we'll be all right out here son, away from the
muck an' the dirt an' the bloody trouble. Eh, I could dance. Come here.

**Mickey** Get off . . .

*Mrs Johnstone picks up a picture of the Pope which is lying next to one of the
suitcases and begins to dance*

**Mrs Johnstone**    Oh, bright new day,
(*singing*)      We're movin' away,
We're startin' all over again.
Oh, bright new day,
We're goin' away,
Where nobody's heard of our name.

(*Speaking*) An' what are you laughin' at?

**Mickey** I'm not laughin'. I'm smilin'. I haven't seen you happy like this for
ages.

**Mrs Johnstone** Well, I am happy now. Eh, Jesus where's the others?

**Mickey** They went into that field, mam.

**Mrs Johnstone** Sammy. SAMMY! Get off that bleedin' cow before I kill
you. Oh Jesus, what's our Donna Marie stepped into? Sammy, that cow's
a bull. Come here the pair of you.

Now we can begin again,
Feel we can win an' then,
Live just like livin' should be.
Got a new situation,
A new destination,
An' no reputation following me.

**All**    We're getting' out. We're movin' house
We're goin' away. Gettin' out today.
We're movin' movin' movin' house.

**Mrs Johnstone**    We're goin' away,
Oh, bright new day.

**CURTAIN**

# ACT II

*As the House Lights go down the introduction for Music 20 begins*

## Music 20: Marilyn Monroe (2)

*Mrs Johnstone moves forward to sing*

**Mrs Johnstone**      The house we got was lovely,
The neighbours are a treat,
They sometimes fight on Saturday night,
But never in the week.

*Mrs Johnstone turns and looks "next door". Raised voices, and a dog barking, are heard, off*

**Neighbours** (*off, speaking*) What time do you call this then?
Time I got shot of you, rat bag!

*Dog barks*

**Mrs Johnstone**      Since I pay me bills on time, the milkman
(*singing*)      Insists I call him Joe.
He brings me bread and eggs

*Joe, the milkman, enters*

Says I've got legs
Like Marilyn Monroe.

*Mrs Johnstone and Joe dance*

Sometimes he takes me dancing
Even takes me dancing.

*Joe exits, dancing*

I know our Sammy burnt the school down
But it's very easily done.
If the teacher lets the silly gets
Play with magnesium.
Thank God he only got probation,

*A Judge is seen, ticking Sammy off*

The Judge was old and slow

*Mrs Johnstone sings to the Judge, laying on a smile for him*

Though it was kind of him,
Said I reminded him of Marilyn Monroe.

**Judge** (*slightly scandalized*) And could I take you dancing?
                      Take you dancing.

*Mrs Johnstone takes the Judge's gavel and bangs him on the head*

   *The Judge exits, stunned*

**Mrs Johnstone**     Our Mickey's just turned fourteen
                    Y'know he's at *that* age

*Mickey is seen in his room*

                    When you mention girls, or courting,
                    He flies into a rage.
**Mickey** (*speaking*) Shut up talking about me, Mother.
**Mrs Johnstone**     He's got a thing for taking blackheads out,
                    And he thinks that I don't know,
                    That he dreams all night of girls who look like
                    Marilyn Monroe. He's even started dancing, secret dancing.

   (*Slower*)      And as for the rest, they've flown the nest
                    Got married or moved away
                    Our Donna Marie's already got three, she's
                    A bit like me that way ...

   (*Slower*)      And that other child of mine,
                    I haven't seen for years, although
                    Each day I pray he'll be OK,
                    Not like Marilyn Monroe ...

*On the other side of the stage Mrs Lyons enters, waltzing with a very awkward fourteen-year-old Edward*

**Mrs Lyons** (*speaking*) One, two, three. One, two three.
   (*Singing*)       Yes, that's right you're dancing.
                    That's right, you're dancing.
   (*Speaking*) You see, Edward, it is easy.
**Edward** It is if you have someone to practice with. Girls. But in term time we hardly ever see a girl, let alone dance with one.
**Mrs Lyons** I'll give you some more lessons when you're home for half term. Now come on, come on, you're going to be late. Daddy's at the door with the car. Now, are you sure you've got all your bags?
**Edward** Yes, they're in the boot.
**Mrs Lyons** (*looking at him*) I'll see you at half term then, darling. (*She kisses him, a light kiss, but holds on to him*) Look after yourself my love.
**Edward** Oh Mummy ... stop fussing ... I'm going to be late.
**Mrs Lyons** We have had a very good time this holiday though, haven't we?
**Edward** We always do.
**Mrs Lyons** Yes. We're safe here, aren't we?
**Edward** Mummy what are you on about? Sometimes ...

*A car horn is heard (see Vocal Score)*

**Mrs Lyons** (*hustling him out, good naturedly*) Go on, go on ... There's Daddy getting impatient. Bye, bye, Edward.
**Edward** Bye, Ma.

*Edward exits*

*We see Mrs Johnstone hustling Mickey to school*

**Mrs Johnstone** You're gonna be late y' know. Y' late already.
**Mickey** I'm not.
**Mrs Johnstone** You're gonna miss the bus.
**Mickey** I won't.
**Mrs Johnstone** Well, you'll miss Linda, she'll be waitin' for y'.
**Mickey** Well, I don't wanna see her. What do I wanna see her for?
**Mrs Johnstone** (*laughing at his transparency*) You've only been talkin' about her in your sleep for the past week ...
**Mickey** (*outraged*) You liar ...
**Mrs Johnstone** "Oh, my sweet darling ..."
**Mickey** I never. That was—a line out the school play!
**Mrs Johnstone** (*her laughter turning to a smile*) All right. I believe y'. Now go before you miss the bus. Are y' goin'.

*We see Linda at the bus stop*

**Linda** Hi-ya, Mickey.
**Mrs Johnstone** Ogh, did I forget? Is that what you're waitin' for? Y' waitin' for y' mum to give y' a big sloppy kiss, come here ...
**Mickey** I'm goin, I'm goin' ...

*Sammy runs through the house, pulling on a jacket as he does so*

**Sammy** Wait for me, YOU.
**Mrs Johnstone** Where you goin' Sammy?
**Sammy** (*on his way out*) The dole.

*Micky and Sammy exit*

*Mrs Johnstone stands watching them as they approach the bus stop. She smiles at Mickey's failure to cope with Linda's smile of welcome*

*The "bus" appears, with the Narrator as the conductor*

**Conductor** Come on, if y' gettin' on. We've not got all day.

*Sammy, Mickey and Linda get on the "bus"*

**Mrs Johnstone** (*calling to her kids*) Tarrah, lads. Be good, both of y' now. I'll cook a nice surprise for y' tea.
**Conductor** (*noticing her as he goes to ring the bell*) Gettin' on, Missis?

**Music 21: Underscoring**

*Mrs Johnstone shakes her head, still smiling*

(*Speaking*)          Happy are y'. Content at last?
                            Wiped out what happened, forgotten the past?

*She looks at him, puzzled*

But you've got to have an endin', if a start's been made.
No one gets off without the price bein' paid.

*The "bus" pulls away as the conductor begins to collect fares*

No one can embark without the price bein' paid.

(*To Mickey*) Yeh?
**Mickey** (*handing over his money*) A fourpenny scholar.
**Conductor** How old are y'?
**Linda** He's fourteen. Both of us are. A fourpenny scholar for me as well.

*The conductor gives out the tickets as Sammy offers his money*

**Sammy** Same for me.
**Conductor** No son.
**Sammy** What?
**Conductor** You're older than fourteen.
**Mickey** (*worried*) Sammy ...
**Sammy** Shut it. (*To the conductor*) I'm fourteen. I wanna fourpenny scholar.
**Conductor** Do you know the penalty for tryin' to defraud ...
**Sammy** I'm not defraudin' no one.
**Conductor** (*shouting to the driver*) 'Ey, Billy, take the next left will y'. We've got one for the cop shop here.
**Sammy** What? (*He stands*)
**Mickey** He didn't mean it, Mister. Don't be soft. He, he was jokin'. Sammy tell him, tell him you're really sixteen. I'll lend you the rest of the fare ...
**Sammy** (*considers; then*) Fuck off (*He produces a knife. To the conductor*) Now move, you. Move! Give me the bag.

### Music 22: Underscoring

**Mickey** Sammy ... Sammy ...
**Sammy** (*to the conductor*) I said give. Stop the bus.

*The conductor rings the bell to stop the "bus"*

Come on, Mickey.
**Linda** You stay where y' are, Mickey. You've done nothin'.
**Mickey** Sammy, Sammy put that away ... it's still not to late. (*To the conductor*) Is it, Mister?
**Sammy** Mickey.
**Linda** He's stayin' here.
**Sammy** No-mark!

*Sammy leaps from the "bus" and is pursued by two policemen*

*The "bus" pulls away leaving Mickey and Linda alone on the pavement*

**Linda** He'll get put away for this, y' know, Mickey.
**Mickey** I know.
**Linda** He's always been a soft get, your Sammy.
**Mickey** I know.

**Linda**  You better hadn't do anything soft, like him.
**Mickey**  I wouldn't.
**Linda**  Y' better hadn't or I won't be in love with y' anymore!
**Mickey**  Shut up! Y' always sayin' that.
**Linda**  I'm not.
**Mickey**  Yis y'are. Y' bloody well said it in assembly yesterday.
**Linda**  Well. I was only tellin' y'.
**Mickey**  Yeh, an' five hundred others as well.
**Linda**  I don't care who knows. I just love you. I love you!
**Mickey**  Come on . . . we're half an hour late as it is.

### Music 23: Underscoring

*Mickey hurries off, followed by Linda*

*The Lights crossfade to Edward's school where Edward is confronted by a teacher (the Narrator) looking down his nose at Edward*

**Teacher**  You're doing very well here, aren't you, Lyons?
**Edward**  Yes, sir. I believe so.
**Teacher**  Talk of Oxbridge.
**Edward**  Yes, sir.
**Teacher**  Getting rather big for your boots, aren't you?
**Edward**  No, sir.
**Teacher**  No, sir? Yes, sir. I think you're a tyke, Lyons. The boys in your dorm say you wear a locket around your neck. Is that so?

*Pause*

**Edward**  Yes, sir.
**Teacher**  A locket? A locket. This is a boys' school, Lyons.
**Edward**  I am a boy, sir.
**Teacher**  Then you must behave like one. Now give this locket to me.
**Edward**  No, sir.
**Teacher**  No sir? Am I to punish you Lyons? Am I to have you flogged?
**Edward**  You can do exactly as you choose Sir. You can take a flying fuck at a rolling doughnut! But you shall not take my locket!
**Teacher**  (*thunderstruck*) I'm going to . . . I'm going to have you suspended, Lyons.
**Edward**  Yes, sir.

*Edward exits*

*As Edward exits a class in a Secondary Modern school is formed—all boredom and futility. The school bell rings. The teacher becomes the teacher of this class in which we see Linda and Mickey*

**Teacher**  And so, we know then, don't we, that the Boro Indian of the Amazon Basin lives on a diet of . . .
**Perkins**  Sir, sir . . .
**Teacher**  A diet of . . .
**Perkins**  Sir, sir . . .

**Teacher** A diet of what, Johnstone! The Boro Indian of the Amazon Basin lives on a diet of what?

**Mickey** What?

**Teacher** Exactly lad, exactly. What?

**Mickey** I don't know.

**Teacher** (*his patience gone*) Y'don't know. (*Mimicking*) You don't know. I told y' two minutes ago, lad.

**Linda** Leave him alone will y'.

**Teacher** You just stay out of this, Miss. It's got nothing to do with you. It's Johnstone, not you ...

**Perkins** Sir!

**Teacher** Oh, shut up Perkins, y' borin' little turd. But you don't listen do you, Johnstone?

**Mickey** (*shrugging*) Yeh.

**Teacher** Oh, y' do? Right, come out here in front of the class. Now then, what is the staple diet of the Boro Indian of the Amazon Basin?

*Mickey looks about for help. There is none*

**Mickey** (*defiantly*) Fish Fingers!

**Teacher** Just how the hell do you hope to get a job when you never listen to anythin'?

**Mickey** It's borin'.

**Teacher** Yes, yes, you might think it's boring but you won't be sayin' that when you can't get a job.

**Mickey** Yeh. Yeh an' it'll really help me to get a job if I know what some soddin' pygmies in Africa have for their dinner!

*The class erupts into laughter*

**Teacher** (*to class*) Shut up. Shut up.

**Mickey** Or maybe y' were thinkin' I was lookin' for a job in an African restaurant.

**Teacher** Out!

**Linda** Take no notice Mickey. I love you.

**Teacher** Johnstone, get out!

**Linda** Oh, leave him alone you. Y' big worm!

**Teacher** Right you as well ... out ... out ...

**Linda** I'm goin' ... I'm goin' ...

**Teacher** You're both suspended.

*Linda and Mickey leave the class*

*The Lights crossfade to the Lyons house*

*The classroom sequence breaks up as we see Mrs Lyons staring at a piece of paper. Edward is standing before her*

**Mrs Lyons** (*incredulously*) Suspended? Suspended? (*She looks at the paper*) Because of a locket?

**Edward** Because I wouldn't let them have my locket.

**Mrs Lyons** But what's so ... Can I see this locket?

*There is a pause*

**Edward** I suppose so . . . if you want to.

*Edward takes off the locket from around his neck and hands it to his mother. She looks at it without opening it*

**Mrs Lyons** Where did you get this?
**Edward** I can't tell you that. It's a secret.
**Mrs Lyons** (*finally smiling in relief*) I know it's from a girlfriend, isn't it? (*She laughs*) Is there a picture in here?
**Edward** Yes, Mummy. Can I have it back now?
**Mrs Lyons** You won't let Mummy see your girl friend. Oh, Edward, don't be so . . . (*She playfully moves away*) Is she beautiful?
**Edward** Mummy can . . .
**Mrs Lyons** Oh, let me look, let me look. (*She beams a smile at him and then opens the locket*)

### Music 24: Underscoring

**Edward** Mummy . . . Mummy what's wrong . . . (*He goes to her and holds her steady*) Mummy!

*Mrs Lyons takes his arms away from her*

What is it?
**Mrs Lyons** When . . . when were you photographed with this woman?
**Edward** Pardon!
**Mrs Lyons** When! Tell me, Edward.

*Edward begins to laugh*

Edward!
**Edward** Mummy . . . you silly old thing. That's not me. That's Mickey.
**Mrs Lyons** What?
**Edward** Mickey . . . you remember my friend when I was little. (*He takes the locket and shows it to her*) Look. That's Mickey . . . and his mother. Why did you think it was me? (*He looks at it*) I never looked a bit like Mickey.

*Edward replaces the locket around his neck. Mrs Lyons watches him*

**Mrs Lyons** No it's just . . . (*She stares, deep in thought*)
**Edward** (*looking at her*) Are you feeling all right Mummy? You're not ill again, like you used to be . . . are you?
**Mrs Lyons** Where did you get that . . . locket from, Edward? Why do you wear it?
**Edward** I can't tell you that, Ma. I've explained, it's a secret, I can't tell you.
**Mrs Lyons** But . . . but I'm your mother.
**Edward** I know but I still can't tell you. It's not important, I'm going up to my room. It's just, just a secret, everybody has secrets, don't you have secrets?

*Edward exits to his room*

*The Lights fade to a spot*

*The Narrator enters*

**Music 24** (continue)

**Narrator**          Did you really feel that you'd become secure
(*singing*)           That time had brushed away the past
                      That there's no one by the window, no one knocking on
                          your door
                      Did you believe that you were free at last
                      Free from the broken looking glass.

                      Oh y' know the devil's got your number
                      He's never far behind you
                      He always knows where to find you
                      And someone said they'd seen him walking past your
                          door

*As the Lights change the music segues into No. 25*

*We see Mickey and Linda making their way up the hill. Linda having some
difficulty in high heeled shoes*

**Linda** Tch . . . you didn't tell me it was gonna be over a load of fields.
**Mickey** I didn't tell y' nothin'. I didn't ask y' to come, y' followed me'. (*He
walks away from her*)
**Linda** (*watching him walk away*) Mickey, Mickey . . . I'm stuck . . . (*Holding
out her helpless arms*) Me foot's stuck. Honest.

*Mickey goes back, timidly takes a wrist and ineffectually pulls*

     Mickey, I think y' might be more successful if you were to sort of put your
     arms around here. (*She puts his hands on her waist*) Oh, Mickey, be gentle,
     be gentle . . .
**Mickey** (*managing to pull her free*) Will you stop takin' the piss out of me!
**Linda** I'm not, I'm not.

*Mickey points down in the direction they have come from*

**Mickey** Look . . . y'can see the estate from up here.
**Linda** Have we come all this way just to look at the bleedin' estate? Mickey
     we're fourteen.

*She beams at him. He can't take it and looks the other way*

**Mickey** Look.
**Linda** What?
**Mickey** There's that lad lookin' out the window. I see him sometimes when
     I'm up here.
**Linda** Oh him . . . he's gorgeous, isn't he?
**Mickey** What?
**Linda** He's lovely lookin', isnt he?
**Mickey** All right, all right! You've told me once.

**Linda** Well, he is. An' what do you care if I think another feller's gorgeous eh?

**Mickey** I don't.

**Linda** You . . . I give up with you, Mickey Johnstone. I'm off. You get on my bleedin' nerves.

*Linda exits*

**Mickey** What . . . Linda . . . Linda . . . Don't . . . Linda, I wanna kiss y', an' put me arms around y' an' kiss y' and kiss y' an' even fornicate with y' but I don't know how to tell y', because I've got pimples an' me feet are too big an' me bum sticks out an' . . .

*He becomes conscious of Edward approaching, and affects nonchalance*

**Music 26: That Guy**

| | |
|---|---|
| (*Speaking*) | If I was like him |
| | I'd know (*singing*) all the right words |
| **Edward** | If I was like . . . him |
| | I'd know some real birds |
| | Apart from those in my dreams |
| | And in magazines. |
| **Mickey** | Just look at his hair |
| **Edward** | His hair's dark and wavy |
| | Mine's mousey to fair |
| **Mickey** | Mine's the colour of gravy |
| **Edward** \| (*together*) \| | Each part of his face |
| **Mickey** \| | Is in just the right place, is |
| | He laughing at me |
| | At my nose, did he notice |
| **Mickey** | I should wear a brace |
| **Edward** | That I've got halitosis |
| **Mickey** \| (*together*) \| | When nature picked on me |
| **Edward** \| | She chose to stick on me |
| **Edward** | Eyes that don't match |
| **Mickey** | And ears that stand out |
| **Edward** \| (*together*) \| | She picked the wrong batch |
| **Mickey** \| | When she handed mine out |
| | And then she attacked me |
| | With permanent acne |
| **Edward** | I wish I was a bit like |
| | Wish that I could score a hit like |
| | And be just a little bit like |
| | That guy |
| | That guy |
| **Mickey** | I wish that I could be like |
| | Just a little less like me |
| | Like the sort of guy I see, like |
| | That guy |
| | That guy. |

**Edward** Hi.

**Mickey** Hi. Gis a ciggie?

**Edward** Oh, I don't smoke actually. But I can go and get you some.

**Mickey** Are you soft? (*He suddenly realizes*) A blood brother.

**Edward** Mickey? Well, shag the vicar.

*Mickey laughs*

What's wrong?

**Mickey** You, it sounds dead funny swearin' in that posh voice.

**Edward** What posh voice?

**Mickey** That one.

**Edward** Well, where do you live?

**Mickey** The estate, look. (*He points*)

**Edward** My God, I only live . . .

**Mickey** I know.

**Edward** That girl I saw you with, was that . . .

**Mickey** Linda. Do you remember Linda?

**Edward** Wow, was that Linda? And is she your girl friend?

**Mickey** Yeh. She's one of them.

**Edward** One of them.

**Mickey** Have you got a girl friend?

**Edward** Me? Me? No!

**Mickey** Haven't y'?

**Edward** Look, you seem to have rather a lot of them, erm . . . perhaps you'd share one with me.

**Mickey** Share one. Eddie I haven't even got one girl friend.

**Edward** But Linda . . . you said . . .

**Mickey** I know, but she's not. I mean, I mean she would be me girl friend, she even says she loves me all over the place, but it's just like dead difficult.

**Edward** What?

**Mickey** Like knowing what to say.

**Edward** But you must, you must . . .

**Mickey** I know that. But every time I see her I promise meself I'll ask her but, but the words just disappear.

**Edward** But you mustn't let them.

**Mickey** What do I say, though?

**Edward** Mickey, it's easy, I've read about it. Look the next time you see Linda, you stare straight into her eyes and you say, "Linda, I love you, I want you, the very core of my being is longing for you, my loins are burning for you. Let me lay my weary head between your warm breasts! And then, Mickey, her eyes will be half closed and her voice may appear somewhat husky as she pleads with you, 'be gentle with me, be gentle'." It would work, you know. Listen, we can see how it's done; look, the Essoldo for one week only, *Nymphomaniac Nights* and *Swedish Au Pairs*. Whoa . . .

**Mickey** I'll have to go home and get some money . . .

*During the next three lines, as the boys are going, we see Mrs Lyons appear. She has seen Edward with Mickey and she stares after them. Making up her mind she quickly goes and fetches a coat, then follows the two boys*

*The Narrator enters*

### Music 27: Shoes Upon The Table (reprise)

**Edward** I've got plenty, I'll lend ...
**Mickey** No, it's all right, me Mam'll give it me ...
**Edward** Come on then, before my Ma sees me. She's off her beam, my Ma ...

*The boys exit, followed by Mrs Lyons*

**Narrator**          Did you really feel that you'd become secure,
(*singing*)           And that the past was tightly locked away,
                      Did you really feel that you would never be found,
                      Did you forget you've got some debts to pay,
                      Did you forget about the reckoning day.

                      Yes, the devil he's still got your number,
                      He's moved in down the street from you,
                      Someone said he wants to speak to you,
                      Someone said they'd seen him leanin' on your door.

*The Narrator exits*

*The Lights crossfade to the Johnstone house*

*We see Mrs Johnstone in her kitchen as Mickey bursts in followed by Edward*

**Mickey** Mother, mam, look, look it's Eddie ... Eddie ...

*Mrs Johnstone stands looking at Edward and smiling*

**Edward** Hi-ya, Mrs Johnstone. Isn't it fantastic. We're neighbours again.
**Mickey** Mum, mum, mum, Eddie lives in that house, y' know that big house on the hill. Mam, can y' lend us a quid to go to the pictures ...
**Mrs Johnstone** Yeh, it's, erm ... it's in the sideboard ...
**Mickey** Oh thanks, mam. I love y'.

*Mickey exits to the next room*

**Edward** You're looking very well, Mrs Johnstone.
**Mrs Johnstone** Am I? Do you ... Do you still keep that locket I gave y'?
**Edward** Of course ... Look ...

*Mickey enters*

**Mickey** Mam, Mam, can I bring Eddie back afterwards, for coffee?
**Mrs Johnstone** Yeh. Go on ... go an' enjoy yourselves but don't be too late will y'?

**Mickey** See y, Mam ...
**Edward** Bye Mrs Johnstone.

*The boys prepare to leave*

**Mrs Johnstone** 'Ey. What's the film you're gonna see?
**Edward** Erm what?
**Mrs Johnstone** What film ...
**Edward** } *(together)* { *Dr Zhivago*
**Mickey** } *(together)* { *Magnificent Seven*
**Mrs Johnstone** Dr Zhivago's Magnificent Seven.
**Edward** It's a double bill.
**Mrs Johnstone** I see. An' where's it on?
**Mickey** } *(together)* { WHAT?
**Edward** } *(together)* { The Essoldo
**Mrs Johnstone** Oh ... the Essoldo eh? When I passed the Essoldo this
    mornin' they were showin' *Nymphomaniac Nights* and *Swedish Au Pairs*.
**Edward** Ah yes, Mrs Johnstone, yes, yes they're just the trailers: a documen-
    tary and and ...
**Mickey** An' a travelogue. About Sweden!
**Mrs Johnstone** Do the pair of you really think I was born yesterday?

*Edward can't hold it any longer and breaks into embarrassed laughter*

**Mickey** *(trying to hold on)* It is, it is ... it's just a travelogue ...
**Mrs Johnstone** Showing the spectacular bends and curves of Sweden ... Go
    on y' randy little sods ...
**Mickey** *(scandalized)* Mother!
**Mrs Johnstone** Go on before I throw a bucket of water over the pair
    of y' ...

*Mickey drags Edward out*

    I don't know about coffee ... you'd be better off with bromide. (*She gets
    on with her work*)
**Edward** *(outside the house but looking back)* She's fabulous your ma, isn't
    she?
**Mickey** She's a fuckin' head case. Come on ...

### Music 28: Underscoring

*As they run off we see Mrs Lyons appear from where she has been concealed
in the alley*

*Mrs Johnstone is lilting the "We Go Dancing" line as Mrs Lyons appears in
the kitchen. Mrs Johnstone gets a shock as she looks up and sees Mrs Lyons
there. The two women stare at each other*

**Mrs Johnstone** *(eventually nodding)* Hello.
**Mrs Lyons** How long have you lived here?

*Pause*

**Mrs Johnstone** A few years.

*Pause*

**Mrs Lyons**  Are you always going to follow me?

**Mrs Johnstone**  We were rehoused here ... I didn't follow ...

**Mrs Lyons**  Don't lie! I know what you're doing to me! You gave him that locket didn't you? Mm?

*Mrs Johnstone nods*

He never takes it off you know. You're very clever aren't you?

**Mrs Johnstone**  I ... I thought I'd never see him again. I wanted him to have ... a picture of me ... even though he'd never know.

**Mrs Lyons**  Afraid he might eventually have forgotten you? Oh no. There's no chance of that. He'll always remember you. After we'd moved he talked less and less of you and your family. I started ... just for a while I came to believe that he was actually mine.

**Mrs Johnstone**  He is yours.

**Mrs Lyons**  No. I took him. But I never made him mine. Does he know? Have you told ...

**Mrs Johnstone**  Of course not!

**Mrs Lyons**  Even when—when he was a tiny baby I'd see him looking straight at me and I'd think, he knows ... he knows. (*Pause*) You have ruined me. (*Pause*) But you won't ruin Edward! Is it money you want?

**Mrs Johnstone**  What?

**Mrs Lyons**  I'll get it for you. If you move away from here. How much?

**Mrs Johnstone**  Look ...

**Mrs Lyons**  How much?

**Mrs Johnstone**  Nothin! Nothing. (*Pause*) You bought me off once before ...

**Mrs Lyons**  Thousands ... I'm talking about thousands if you want it? And think what you could do with money like that.

**Mrs Johnstone**  I'd spend it. I'd buy more junk and trash; that's all. I don't want your money. I've made a life out here. It's not much of one maybe, but I made it. I'm stayin' here. You move if you want to.

**Mrs Lyons**  I would. But there's no point. You'd just follow me again wouldn't you?

**Mrs Johnstone**  Look, I'm not followin' anybody.

**Mrs Lyons**  Wherever I go you'll be just behind me. I know that now ... always and forever and ever like, like a shadow ... unless I can ... make ... you go ... But you won't so ...

*We see that throughout the above Mrs Lyons has opened the knife drawer and has a lethal-looking kitchen knife in her hand. Mrs Johnstone, unaware, has her back to her. On impulse, and punctuated by a note, Mrs Johnstone wheels. On a punctuated note Mrs Lyons lunges. Mrs Johnstone moves and avoids it. Mrs Lyons lunges again but Mrs Johnstone manages to get hold of her wrist, rendering the knife hand helpless. Mrs Johnstone takes the knife from Mrs Lyons's grasp and moves away*

**Mrs Johnstone** (*staring at her; knowing*) YOU'RE MAD. MAD.

**Mrs Lyons** (*quietly*) I curse the day I met you. You ruined me.
**Mrs Johnstone** Go. Just go!
**Mrs Lyons** Witch (*Suddenly pointing*) I curse you. Witch!
**Mrs Johnstone** (*screaming*) Go!

*Mrs Lyons exits to the street*

*Kids voices are heard, chanting, off*

**Kids** (*off*)          High upon the hill the mad woman lives,
                          Never ever eat the sweets she gives,
                          Just throw them away and tell your Dad,
                          High upon a hill there's a woman gone mad.

                          Mad woman, mad woman living on the hill,
                          If she catches your eye then you never will
                          Grow any further, your teeth will go bad
                          High upon a hill there's a woman gone mad.

**Music 29: Underscoring** (as required)
*Eddie and Mickey emerge from the cinema, blinking as they try to adjust to
the glare of the light in the street*

*They are both quite overcome with their celluloid/erotic encounter. As they
pause and light up cigarettes by a corner lamp post they groan in their ecstatic
agony. Each is in an aroused trance*

**Mickey** Ooh . . . !
**Edward** Naked knockers, ooh . . .!
**Mickey** Naked knockers with nipples . . .
**Edward** Playing tennis. Ooh. Tennis with tits. Will Wimbledon ever be the
same.
**Mickey** Tits!
**Edward** Tits, tits, tits . . . (*He begins a frustrated chant of the word, oblivious
to everything*)

*Linda and a mate enter*

*Finally Mickey realizes Linda's presence and knocks Edward, who becomes
aware of the girls' presence. He goes into a song without missing a beat*

                          Tits, tits, tits a lovely way,
                          To spend an evening. . .

*Edward grabs Linda's protesting mate and begins to waltz her around the
street*

                          Can't think of anything
                          I'd rather do . . .

**Mate** (*simultaneously with the above*) Gerroff. Put me down, get y' friggin'
paws off me you. Linda. Y' bloody lunatic, gettoff.

*Edward finally releases her and bows*

Linda, come on. I'm goin' ...

*The mate begins to walk away. Linda makes no attempt to follow*

**Linda** What y' doin' in town, Mick?
**Mickey** We've erm, we've ...
**Edward** We have been undergoing a remarkable celluloid experience!
**Mate** We'll miss the bus, Linda.
**Mickey** We've been the pictures.
**Linda** So have we. What did y' go see?
**Edward** *Nympho ...*
**Mickey** *Bridge Over the River Kwai.*
**Linda** Ah, we've seen that. We went to see *Nymphomaniac Nights* instead.
An' *Swedish Au Pairs.*
**Mickey** You what!

*Edward begins to laugh*

**Mate** Oh, sod y' then. I'm goin'.

*The mate exits*

**Mickey** (*to Edward*) What are you laughin' at? Take no notice. Remember
Eddie? He's still a head case. Shurrup.
**Edward** (*shouting*) Tits. Tits, tits, tits, tits, tits.

*Edward leaps around and hopefully ends up sitting at the top of the lamp post.
Linda and Mickey laugh at him, while Edward chants*

*A Policeman enters*

*The three do not see the arrival of the Policeman*

**Policeman** An' what the bloody hell do you think you're doin'?
**Edward** Adolph Hitler?
**Policeman** Get down.

*Edward gets down from the lamp post*

**Policeman** (*getting out his black book*) Right. I want your names. What's
your name?
**Linda**
**Mickey** (*together*) Waitin' for the ninety-two bus!
**Edward**
**Linda** (*pointing upwards*) Oh my God, look ...
**Policeman** Now listen ...

*The Policeman falls for it and looks up*

*The three make their exit*

*The Policeman realizes and gives chase*

*Mickey, Linda and Edward enter, laughing and exhausted*

*The Narrator enters*

**Narrator**         There's a few bob in your pocket and you've got good
                     friends,
               And it seems that Summer's never coming to an end,
               Young, free and innocent, you haven't got a care,
               Apart from decidin' on the clothes you're gonna wear.
               The street's turned into Paradise, the radio's singing
                   dreams
               You're innocent, immortal, you're just fifteen.

*The Lights crossfade to the fairground*

*The Narrator becomes the rifle range man at the fairground*

  *Linda, Mickey and Edward rush on*

*Linda, Mickey and Edward pool their money and hand it to the rifle range
man. He gives the gun to Mickey, who smiles, shakes his head and points to
Linda. The man offers the gun to Edward but Linda takes it. The boys indicate
to the rifle range man that he has had it now Linda has the gun. They eagerly
watch the target but their smiles fade as Linda misses all three shots. Mickey
and Edward turn on Linda in mock anger. They are stopped by the rifle range
man throwing them a coconut which is used as a ball for a game of piggy-in-
the-middle. When Linda is caught in the middle the game freezes*

        (*Picking up the rifle*)
               And who'd dare tell the lambs in Spring,
               What fate the later seasons bring.
               Who'd tell the girl in the middle of the pair
               The price she'll pay for just being there.

*He relents and laughs as the frame unfreezes*

*Throughout the following we see Linda, Mickey and Edward suiting their
action to the words—coming out of the chip shop, talking, lighting a cigarette
by the lamp post*

               But leave them alone, let them go and play
               They care not for what's at the end of the day.
               For what is to come, for what might have been,
               Life has no ending when you're sweet sixteen
               And your friends are with you to talk away the night,
               Or until Mrs Wong switches off the chippy light.
               Then there's always the corner and the street lamp's glare
               An' another hour to spend, with your friends, with her,
               To share your last cigarette and your secret dream
               At the midnight hour, at seventeen.

*Throughout the following we see Linda, Mickey and Edward, as if at the
beach, Linda taking a picture of Mickey and Edward, arms around each other
camping it for the camera but eventually giving good and open smiles. Mickey
taking a picture of Edward and Linda. Edward down on one knee and kissing
her hand Edward taking a picture of Mickey and Linda. Mickey pulling a*

*distorted face, Linda wagging a finger at him. Mickey chastened. Linda raising her eyebrows and putting one of his arms round her. Linda moving forward and taking the camera. Linda waving the Narrator to snap them. He goes. Linda showing the Narrator how to operate the camera. Linda, Mickey and Edward, grouped together, arms around each other as the Narrator takes the picture. They get the camera and wave their thanks to the Narrator*

It's just another ferry boat, a trip to the beach
But everything is possible, the world's within your reach
An' you don't even notice broken bottles in the sand
The oil in the water and you can't understand
How living could be anything other than a dream
When you're young, free and innocent and just eighteen.

*Linda, Mickey and Edward exit*

*The Lights fade to a spot on the Narrator*

And only if the three of them could stay like that forever,
And only if we could predict no changes in the weather,
And only if we didn't live in life, as well as dreams
And only if we could stop and be forever, just eighteen.

*The Lights come upon a street*

*We see Edward, waiting by a street lamp*

*Linda approaches, sees him, and goes into a street walk*

**Linda** Well, hallo, sweetie pie; looking for a good time? Ten to seven (*She laughs*) Good time ... ten to seven ... it was a joke ... I mean I know it was a lousy joke but y' could at least go into hysterics!

*Edward smiles*

That's hysterics?
**Edward** Where's Mickey?
**Linda** He must be workin' overtime.
**Edward** Oh.
**Linda** What's wrong with you, misery?
**Edward** (*after a pause*) I go away to university tomorrow.
**Linda** Tomorrow! You didn't say.
**Edward** I know. I think I've been pretending that if I didn't mention it the day would never come. I love it when we're together, the three of us, don't you?

*Linda nods*

Can I write to you?
**Linda** Yeh ... yeh, if you want.
**Edward** Would Mickey mind?
**Linda** Why should he?
**Edward** Come on ... because you're his girl friend.

**Linda** No, I'm not.
**Edward** You are, Linda.
**Linda** I'm not, he hasn't asked me.
**Edward** (*laughing*) You mean he still hasn't?
**Linda** (*laughing*) No.
**Edward** But it's ridiculous.
**Linda** I know. I hope for his sake he never has to ask me to marry him. He'll
be a pensioner before he gets around to it.
**Edward** (*after a pause*) He's mad. If I was Mickey I would have asked you
years ago.
**Linda** I know *you* would. Cos y' soft you are.

### Music 30: I'm Not Saying A Word

**Edward**              If I could stand inside his shoes I'd say,
(*singing*)              How can I compare thee to a summer's day
**Linda** (*speaking*) Oh go away ...
**Edward**              I'd take a page in all the papers, I'd announce it on the
news
If I was the guy, if I
Was in his shoes.

If I was him I'd bring you flowers
And ask you to dance
We'd while away the hours making future plans
For rainy days in country lanes
And trips to the sea
I'd just tell you that I love you
If it was me

But I'm not saying a word,
I'm not saying I care,
Though I would like you to know,
That I'm not saying a word,
I'm not saying I care,
Though I would like you to know.

If I was him I'd have to tell you,
What I've kept in my heart,
That even if we had to live
Some worlds apart
There would not be a day
In which I'd not think of you
If I was him, if I was him
That's what I'd do

But I'm not saying a word
I'm not saying I care
Though I would like you to know

> That I'm not saying a word
> I'm not saying I care
> Though I would like you to know

**Edward** But I'm not.
**Linda** What?
**Edward** Mickey.

*Mickey enters*

Mickey!
**Mickey** Hi-ya, Ed. Lind.
**Linda** Where've y' been?
**Mickey** I had to do overtime. I hate that soddin' place.
**Edward** Mickey. I'm going away tomorrow ... to University.
**Mickey** What? Y' didn't say.
**Edward** I know ... but the thing is I won't be back until Christmas. Three months. Now you wouldn't want me to continue in suspense for all that time would you?
**Linda** What are you on about?
**Edward** Will you talk to Linda.
**Linda** Oh Eddie ...
**Edward** Go on ... go on.

*Mickey turns and goes to her. Linda tries to keep a straight face*

**Mickey** Erm ... well, the er thing is ... Linda, I've erm ... (*Quickly*) Linda for Christ's sake will you go out with me?
**Linda** (*just as quickly*) Yeh.
**Mickey** Oh ... erm ... Good. Well, I suppose I better ... well er ... come here ... (*He quickly embraces and kisses Linda*)
**Linda** (*fighting for air*) My God. Y' take y' time gettin' goin' but then there's no stoppin' y'.
**Mickey** I know ... come here ...

*They kiss again. Edward turns and begins to leave*

Eddie ... Eddie where y' goin'? I thought we were all goin' the club. There's a dance.
**Edward** No ... I've got to, erm, I've got to pack for tomorrow.
**Mickey** Are y' sure?

*Edward nods*

See y' at Christmas then, Eddie? Listen, I'm gonna do loads of overtime between now and then, so the Christmas party's gonna be on me ... right?
**Edward** Right. It's a deal, Mick. See you.

*Linda rushes across and kisses Edward lightly*

**Linda** Thanks, Eddie.
**Mickey** Yeh, Eddie ... thanks.

*Linda and Mickey, arms around each other, watch him go. They turn and look at each other*

## Music 31: Underscoring

*Mickey and Linda exit*

*The Lights crossfade to the Johnstone house*

*Mickey enters and prepares to go to work*

*Mrs Johnstone enters with Mickey's lunch bag*

*The Narrator enters*

*A spot lights the Narrator*

> It was one day in October when the sun began to fade,
> And Winter broke the promise that Summer had just made,
> It was one day in October when the rain came falling down,
> And someone said the bogey man was seen around the town.

*The Narrator exits*

**Mrs Johnstone** Y' gonna be late Mick. I don't want you gettin' the sack an' spendin' your days idlin' round like our Sammy. Come on.

*Mickey instead of making an effort to go, stands looking at her*

**Mickey** Mam!
**Mrs Johnstone** What?
**Mickey** What!
**Mrs Johnstone** Come on.
**Mickey** Mam. Linda's pregnant!

*A moment*

**Mrs Johnstone** Do you love her?
**Mickey** Yeh!
**Mrs Johnstone** When's the weddin'?
**Mickey** We thought, about a month ... before Christmas anyway. Mam, could we live here for a bit?

*She looks at him and nods*

> Are you mad?

**Mrs Johnstone** At you? Some hypocrite I'd be. No ... I'm not mad son. I'm just thinkin' ... you've not had much of a life with me, have y'?
**Mickey** Don't be stupid, course I have. You're great, you are, Mam. (*He gives her a quick kiss*) Ta-ra I'd better get a move on. They've started layin' people off in the other factory y' know. Tarrah, Mam. Thanks.

*Mickey exits*

## Music 32: Miss Jones

*Mrs Johnstone watches him go. As the underscoring for "Miss Jones" begins she whips off her overall and a wedding suit is underneath. She acquires a hat*

*The Lights become general*

*A wedding party assembles during Verse 1. Mickey remains in his working clothes. Linda is in white. Other guests are suitably attired*

*Mr Lyons enters, as Managing Director, and sings as his secretary, Miss Jones, takes notes*

**Mr Lyons**         Take a letter, Miss Jones (quote)
(*singing*)           I regret to inform you,
                     That owing to circumstances
                     Quite beyond our control.
                     It's a premature retirement
                     For those surplus to requirement,
                     I'm afraid it's a sign of the times,
                     Miss Jones,
                     An unfortunate sign of the times.

*Throughout the next verse we see the wedding party wave goodbye to Mickey who goes to work, only to have his cards given to him when he gets there*

                     Take a letter, Miss Jones,
                     Due to the world situation
                     The shrinking pound, the global slump,
                     And the price of oil
                     I'm afraid we must fire you,
                     We no longer require you,
                     It's just another,
                     Sign of the times,
                     Miss Jones,
                     A most miserable sign of the times

*The Guests at the wedding become a line of men looking for work. Mickey joins them as Linda watches. They are constantly met with shaking heads and by the end of the following verse have assembled in the dole office*

                     Take a letter Miss Jones, of course we'll
                     Let the workforce know when
                     Inflation's been defeated
                     And recession is no more.
                     And for the moment we suggest
                     You don't become too depressed
                     As it's only a sign
                     Of the times,
                     Miss Jones,
                     A peculiar sign of the times.

                     Take a letter Miss Jones:
                     My dear Miss Jones, we'd like to thank you
                     Many years of splendid service,
                     Etcetara blah blah blah
                     You've been a perfect poppet

Yes that's right Miss Jones, you've got it
It's just another sign
Of the times,
Miss Jones, it's
Just another sign of the times

*He shows her the door. Crying she approaches the dole queue but then hesitates. The men in the queue take up the song*

**Doleites**          Dry your eyes, Miss Jones
It's not as bad as it seems (you)
Get used to being idle
In a year or two.
Unemployment's such a pleasure
These days, we call it leisure
It's just another sign
Of the times,
Miss Jones, it's
Just another sign of the times.

*Mickey leaves the group and stands apart. Miss Jones takes his place. Behind Mickey we can see Linda and his Mother*

There's a young man on the street, Miss Jones,
He's walkin' round in circles,
He's old before his time,
But still too young to know.
Don't look at him, don't cry though
This living on the Giro
Is only a sign of the times,
Miss Jones, it's
Just another sign of the times.

*As they exit*

Miss Jones,
It's just another sign of the times ...

*Crowd exits*

*Mickey is left alone, sitting dejected. We hear Christmas Bells*

*Edward enters in a duffle coat and college scarf, unseen by Mickey. Edward creeps up behind Mickey and puts his hands over his eyes*

**Edward** Guess who?
**Mickey** Father Christmas.
**Edward** (*leaping out in front of them*) Mickey ... (*Laughing*) Merry Christmas.

*Mickey, unamused, looks at Edward and then looks away*

Come on then ... I'm back, where's the action, the booze, the Christmas parties, the music and the birds.

*No reaction*

What's wrong, Mickey?

**Mickey** Nothin'. How's University?

**Edward** Mickey, it's fantastic. I haven't been to so many parties in my life. And there's just so many tremendous people, but you'll meet them Mick, some of them, Baz, Ronnie and Clare and oh, lots of them. They're coming over to stay for the New Year, for the party. Ooh it's just . . . it's great, Mickey.

**Mickey** Good.

**Edward** Come on, what's wrong? It's nearly Christmas, we were going to do everything. How's Linda?

**Mickey** She's OK.

**Edward** (*trying again to rally him*) Well, come on then, let's go then . . . come on.

**Mickey** Come on where?

**Edward** Mickey, what's wrong?

**Mickey** You. You're a dick head!

*Edward is slightly unsure but laughs anyway*

There are no parties arranged. There is no booze or music. Christmas? I'm sick to the teeth of Christmas an' it isn't even here yet. See, there's very little to celebrate, Eddie. Since you left I've been walking around all day, every day, lookin' for a job.

**Edward** What about the job you had?

**Mickey** It disappeared (*Pause*) Y' know somethin', I bleedin' hated that job, standin' there all day never doin' nothin' but put cardboard boxes together. I used to get . . . used to get terrified that I'd have to do it for the rest of me life. But, but after three months of nothin', the same answer everywhere, nothin', nothin' down for y'. I'd crawl back to that job for half the pay and double the hours. Just . . . just makin' up boxes it was. But after bein' fucked off from everywhere, it seems like it was paradise.

*Pause*

**Edward** Why . . . why is a job so important? If I couldn't get a job I'd just say, sod it and draw the dole, live like a bohemian, tilt my hat to the world and say "screw you". So you're not working. Why is it so important?

**Mickey** (*looking at him*) You don't understand anythin' do y'? I don't wear a hat that I could tilt at the world.

**Edward** Look . . . come on . . . I've got money, plenty of it. I'm back, let's forget about bloody jobs, let's go and get Linda and celebrate. Look, look, money, lots of it, have some . . . (*He tries to thrust some notes into Mickey's hands*)

**Mickey** No. I don't want your money, stuff it.

*He throws the notes to the ground. Edward picks them up and stands looking at Mickey*

Eddie, just do me a favour an' piss off, will y'?

*Pause*

**Edward** I thought, I thought we always stuck together. I thought we were . . . were blood brothers.

**Mickey** That was kids' stuff, Eddie. Didn't anyone tell y'? (*He looks at Edward*) But I suppose you still are a kid, aren't y'?

**Edward** I'm exactly the same age as you, Mickey.

**Mickey** Yeh. But you're still a kid. An' I wish I could be as well Eddie, I wish I could still believe in all that blood brother stuff. But I can't, because while no one was looking I grew up. An' you didn't, because you didn't need to; an' I don't blame y' for it Eddie. In your shoes I'd be the same, I'd still be able to be a kid. But I'm not in your shoes, I'm in these, lookin' at you. An' you make me sick, right? That was all just kids' stuff, Eddie, an' I don't want to be reminded of it. Right? So just, just take yourself away. Go an' see your friends an' celebrate with them.

*Pause*

Go on . . . beat it before I hit y'.

*Edward looks at Mickey and then slowly backs away*

*Underscoring of "My Best Friend". The Lights change*

*Sammy approaches Mickey as, on the other side, we see Linda hurrying on passing Edward who stops and calls*

**Edward** Linda!
**Sammy** Mickey.
**Edward** Linda.

*Reluctantly she stops, goes back a few paces*

Hello, Linda.

**Linda** Hello, Eddie.

**Edward** Why haven't you called to see me?

**Linda** I heard you had friends, I didn't like butting in.

**Edward** You'd never be butting in and you know it. It wouldn't matter if I never saw those friends again, if I could be with you.

**Linda** Eddie . . .

**Sammy** Look, I'm offerin' . . . all we need is someone to keep the eye for us. Look at y' Mickey. What have y' got? Nothin', like me Mam. Where y' takin' y' tart for New Year? Nowhere.

**Edward** You might as well know, if I'm not going to, see you again. I've always loved you, you must have known that.

**Sammy** We don't *use* the shooters. They're just frighteners. Y' don' need to use them. Everyone behaves when they see a shooter. You won't even be where the action is. Just keep the eye out for us.

**Edward** I'm sorry.

**Sammy** Fifty quid Mickey. Fifty quid for an hour's work. Just think where y' could take Linda if you had cash like that.

**Edward** I'm sorry, Linda.

**Linda** It's all right. I suppose, I suppose I always . . . loved you, in a way.

**Edward** Then marry me.
**Linda** Didn't Mickey tell y'? We got married two weeks before you came home and I'm expecting a baby.
**Mickey** Fifty notes?

*Sammy nods*

All right.
**Sammy** Great.

*Mickey nods*

Cheer up, will y'? It's New Year.

*Sammy exits*

**Edward's Friends** (*variously; off*) Where's Lyo? Come on Lyons, you pillock, you're supposed to be helping us with the booze. Come on Lyolese. Edward, come on.
**Linda** I'll see y' Eddie. Happy New Year. (*She moves away*)

*Edward exits*

**Mickey** Linda ... Linda ...
**Linda** Are you comin' in?
**Mickey** Look ... I'll be back about eight o'clock. An' listen, get dressed up. I'm takin' y' out.
**Linda** What?
**Mickey** We're goin' dancin'. Right? Then we're goin' for a slap-up meal an' tomorrow you can go into town an' get some new clothes.
**Linda** Oh yeh? Where's the money comin' from?
**Mickey** I'm ... doin' some work ...
**Linda** What?
**Mickey** Look, stop arguin', will y'? I'm doin' some work and then I'm takin' you out.
**Sammy** (*off*) Mickey!
**Linda** Is that your Sammy?
**Mickey** Now shut up, Linda. Right, right? Just make sure you're ready at eight ... (*He starts to leave*)
**Linda** (*as he goes*) Mickey ... Mickey ... No!

*Linda exits*

### Music 33: Underscoring

*Mickey moves away*

*The Narrator enters*

*A spot lights the Narrator*

*Sammy enters*

**Narrator**            There's a full moon shining and a joker in the pack,
                         The dealers dealt the cards, and he won't take them back,
                         There's a black cat stalking and a woman who's afraid,
                         That there's no getting off without the price being paid.

*We see Mickey, nervously keeping look-out as behind him, as if inside a filling station office, we see Sammy, his back to us, talking to an off-stage character*

**Sammy** Don't piss about with me, pal . . . I said give! (*Pause*) Listen, it's not a toy y' know . . . We're not playin' games. Y' don't get up again if one of these hits y' . . . What are you doin'? I said listen to me, I said . . . don't you fuckin' touch that . . . Listen.

*An alarm bell is heard, followed by an explosion from the gun. Sammy, reels backwards. He and Mickey run and enter their house*

**Narrator**        There's a man lies bleeding on a garage floor,
**Sammy**           Quick, get in the house an' bolt the fuckin' door.

*Mickey stands unable to move, tears streaming down his face*

**Narrator**        And maybe, if you counted ten and kept your fingers crossed
                    It would all be just a game and then no one would have lost.

**Mickey** You shot him, you shot him.
**Sammy** I know I bloody did.
**Mickey** You shot him, you shot him.
**Sammy** Move, I've got to get this hid.
**Linda** (*off*) Mickey . . . Mickey, is that you?
**Sammy** Ooh, fuck . . . (*He quickly pulls back a mat, pulls up a floorboard and puts the gun beneath it*)

*Linda enters*

*Two Policemen arrive at the house*

*Sammy splits out the back. Mickey remains silently crying. Linda goes to him and puts her arms around him. As Sammy is being apprehended at the back, the other Policeman enters and gently removes Linda from Mickey and leads him out and into the police station*

**Linda** But I've ironed him a shirt.

*The Lights change to the police station and cell*

### Music 34: Marilyn Monroe (3)

*Mickey, placed in a prison cell, stands quietly crying*

*Mrs Johnstone enters*

**Mrs Johnstone**   The jury found him guilty
(*singing*)          Sent him down for seven years,
                    Though he acted like they gave him life,
                    He couldn't stop the tears.
                    And when we went to visit him,
                    He didn't want to know,
                    It seems like jail's sent him off the rails,
                    Just like Marilyn Monroe

His mind's gone dancing
Can't stop dancing

*A doctor enters the cell and examines Mickey*

They showed him to a doctor,
And after routine test,
A prescription note the doctor wrote,
For the chronically depressed.
And now the tears have stopped
He sits and counts the days to go
And treats his ills with daily pills
Just like Marilyn Monroe.

*The doctor exits*

They stop his mind from dancing
Stop it dancing.

*A prison warder leads Linda into the cell. He indicates a seat opposite Mickey*

**Linda** What are y' doin'?
**Mickey** What? I'm takin' me tablet.
**Linda** Listen, Mickey. I've told y'. They're just junk. You'll be home soon, Mickey, and you should come off them.
**Mickey** Why? I need ... I need to take them.
**Linda** Listen, Mickey, you've ...
**Mickey** No! See, he says, the doctor, he said ...
**Linda** What did he say?
**Mickey** He said, about me nerves. An' how I get depressed an' I need to take these cos they make me better ...
**Linda** I get depressed but I don't take those. You don't need those, Mickey.
**Mickey** Leave me alone, will y'? I can't cope with this. I'm not well. The doctor said, didn't he, I'm not well ... I can't do things ... leave me alone ...

*The warder escorts Linda from the cell*

*The Lights change to the Johnstone house*

*Throughout the following verse Mickey leaves the prison and goes home*

**Mrs Johnstone**       With grace for good behaviour
(*singing*)                 He got out before his time
                               The family and the neighbours told him
                               He was lookin' fine.
                               But he's feelin' fifteen years older
                               And his speech is rather slow
                               And the neighbours said
                               You'd think he was dead
                               Like Marilyn Monroe
                               No cause for dancing
                               No more dancing ...

*Linda approaches Mrs Johnstone. Linda is weighed down with shopping bags and is weary*

**Mrs Johnstone** Linda, where've y' been? We've gorra do somethin' about him. He's been out for months and he's still takin' those pills. Linda, he needs a job, you two need a place of your own an' ...

**Linda** Mam ... Mam that's why I'm late, I've been to see ... We're movin' at the end of the month. We've got our own place an' I think I've got Mickey a job ...

**Mrs Johnstone** Oh, Jesus, thank God. But how ...

**Linda** It's all right ... I ... someone I know ...

**Mrs Johnstone** But who ...

**Linda** It's all right Mam. Did y' get our Sarah from school?

**Mrs Johnstone** Yeh, she's in bed, but listen how did y' manage to ...

**Linda** Never mind, Mam. Mam, isn't it great; if he's workin' an' we've got our own place he'll be able to get himself together an' stop takin' those friggin' things ...

*They start to leave*

**Mrs Johnstone** But, listen Linda, who ...

**Linda** Oh just some ... some feller I know. He's ... he's on the housin' committee. You don't know him, Mam ...

*Mrs Johnstone exits*

*The Lights crossfade to Mickey's house. Mickey and Linda are in their new house. In the lounge Linda is preparing Mickey's working things*

(*Shouting*) Mickey, Mickey, come on, you'll be late ...

*Mickey enters his house*

**Mickey** Where's me ...

**Linda** Here ... here's y' bag. Y' sandwiches are in there ...

*He ignores the bag and begins looking through a cupboard drawer*

Mickey, what y' lookin' for?

**Mickey** Y' know what I'm lookin' for.

**Linda** Mickey, Mickey listen to me ...

**Mickey** Where's me tablets gone, Linda?

**Linda** Mickey you don't need your tablets!

**Mickey** Linda!

**Linda** Mickey. You're workin' now, we're livin' on our own—you've got to start makin' an effort.

**Mickey** Give them to me, Linda.

**Linda** You promised.

**Mickey** I know I promised but I can't do without them. I tried. Last week I tried to do without them. By dinner time I was shakin' an' sweating so much I couldn't even work. I need them. That's all there is to it. Now give.

*Pause*

**Linda** Is that it then? Are y' gonna stay on them forever?
**Mickey** Linda.
**Linda** Look. We've ... we've managed to sort ourselves out this far but what's the use if ...
**Mickey** *We* have sorted ourselves out? Do you think I'm really stupid?
**Linda** What?
**Mickey** I didn't sort anythin' out Linda. Not a job, not a house, nothin'. It used to be just sweets an' ciggies he gave me, because I had none of me own. Now it's a job and a house. I'm not stupid, Linda. You sorted it out. You an' Councillor Eddie Lyons.

*Linda doesn't deny it*

Now give me me tablets ... I need them.
**Linda** An' what about what I need? I need you. I love you. But, Mickey, not when you've got them inside you. When you take those things, Mickey, I can't even see you.
**Mickey** That's why I take them. So I can be invisible. (*Pause*) Now give me them.

### Music 35: Light Romance

*As the introduction to "Light Romance" is played we see Linda mutely hand Mickey her bag. Mickey quickly grabs the tablets*

*Mickey exits*

*The Narrator enters*

*The Narrator watches Linda. She moves to telephone, but hesitates*

**Narrator**          There's a girl inside the woman
                      Who's waiting to get free
                      She's washed a million dishes
                      She's always making tea.

**Linda** (*speaking on the 'phone*) Could I talk to Councillor Lyons, please?

**Narrator**          There's a girl inside the woman
                      And the mother she became
                      And a half remembered song
                      Comes to her lips again.

**Linda** (*on the 'phone*) Eddie, could I talk to you? Yeh, I remember.

**Narrator**          The girl would sing the melody
                      But the woman stands in doubt
                      And wonders what the price would be
                      For letting the young girl out.

*Mrs Johnstone enters*

**Mrs Johnstone**     It's just a light romance,
(*singing*)           It's nothing cruel,

> They laid no plans,
> How it came,
> Who can explain?

*The Lights crossfade to the park setting*

*Linda approaches Edward who is waiting at the park fence*

> They just said "hello",
> And foolishly they gazed,
> They should have gone
> Their separate ways

*The music continues*

**Edward** Hey. (*He mimes firing a gun*)
**Linda** Missed.

*Edward laughs, grabbing Linda jokingly. Their smiles fade as they look at each other. Suddenly they kiss. They walk together, hand in hand. All this through the following verse*

**Mrs Johnstone** (*singing*)

> It's just the same old song,
> Nothing cruel,
> Nothing wrong.
> It's just two fools,
> Who know the rules,
> But break them all,
> And grasp at half a chance
> To play their part
> In a light romance.

*The Lights come up on Mickey. Throughout the following chorus we see Mickey at work. We see him go to take his pills. We see him make the effort of not taking them. We see the strain of this upon him but see that he is determined*

> Living on the never never,
> Constant as the changing weather,
> Never sure
> Who's at the door,
> Or the price
> You're gonna have to pay.

*The Lights fade on Mickey as we see Linda and Edward kicking up the leaves before parting*

> It's just a secret glance,
> Across a room.
> A touch of hands
> That part too soon.
> That same old tune

> That always plays,
> And lets them dance as friends,
> Then stand apart,
> As the music ends.

*During the next chorus Edward and Linda wave goodbye, as Edward and Mickey once did. The Lights come up on Mickey, working*

*Mrs Lyons enters and goes to Mickey*

*She turns Mickey round and points out Edward and Linda to him. By the end of the chorus Mickey is hammering on his own door. The Lights come up to full*

> Living on the never never,
> Constant as the changing weather,
> Never sure
> Who's at the door
> Or the price you're gonna have to pay.

*As the music abruptly segues Mickey is heard hammering on his door and calling for Linda, as he once did for his mother. The music pulsates and builds as he runs to his mother's house. He enters and flings back the floorboard to reveal the gun hidden by Sammy*

*Mrs Johnstone enters just as Mickey disappears with the gun*

**Mrs Johnstone** (*screaming*) Mickey ... Mickey ...

*The Narrator continues as we see Mickey comb the town, breaking through groups of people, looking, searching, desperate, not even knowing what he's looking for or what he is going to do. His mother is frantically trying to catch him but not succeeding.*

**Narrator**     There's a man gone mad in the town tonight,
> He's gonna shoot somebody down,
> There's a man gone mad, lost his mind tonight
> There's a mad man
> There's a mad man
> There's a mad man running round and round.
>
> Now you know the devil's got your number,
> He's runnin' right beside you,
> He's screamin' deep inside you,
> And someone said he's callin' your number up today.

*As Mrs Johnstone makes her way to Linda's house the band keep the Narrator company on the line:*

> There's a mad man/There's a mad man/There's a mad man

*Which runs under the following:*

*Mrs Johnstone hammers on Linda's door, shouting her name. Linda, just returning home, comes up behind her*

**Linda** Mam ... Mam ... what's ...
**Mrs Johnstone** (*out of breath*) He's ... Mickey ... Mickey's got a gun ...
**Linda** Mickey? ... Eddie? ... The Town Hall ...
**Mrs Johnstone** What?
**Linda** (*beginning to run*) Eddie Lyons!

*A sudden spotlight on Mrs Johnstone shows her to be terrified*

**Narrator**              There's a mad man running round and round
                          You know the devil's got your number
                          You know he's right beside you
                          He's screamin' deep inside you
                          And someone said he's callin' your number up today
                          Today
                          Today
                          TODAY!

*On the last three words of the chorus Mrs Johnstone runs off*

*On the last "Today" the music stops abruptly*

*The Lights change . We see Edward, standing behind a table, on a platform.
He is in the middle of addressing his audience. Two Councillors stand either
side*

**Edward** And if, for once, I agree with Councillor Smith, you mustn't hold
  that against me. But in this particular instance, yes, I do agree with him.
  You're right, Bob, there is light at the end of the tunnel. Quite right. None
  of us would argue with you on that score. But what we would question is
  this, how many of us ...

*From his audience a commotion beginning. He thinks he is being heckled and
so tries to carry on. In fact his audience is reacting to the sight of Mickey
appearing from the stalls, a gun held two-handed, to steady his shaking hands,
and pointed directly at Edward. Edward turns and see Mickey as someone on
the platform next to him realizes the reality of the situation and screams*

**Mickey** Stay where you are!

*Mickey stops a couple of yards from Edward. He is unsteady and breathing
awkwardly*

**Edward** (*eventually*) Hello, Mickey.
**Mickey** I stopped takin' the pills.
**Edward** (*pause*) Oh.
**Mickey** (*eventually*) I began thinkin' again. Y'see. (*To the Councillor*) Just
  get her out of here, mister, now!

  *The Councillors hurry off*

*Edward and Mickey are now alone on the platform*

  I had to start thinkin' again. Because there was one thing left in my life.
  (*Pause*) Just one thing I had left, Eddie—Linda—an' I wanted to keep
  her. So, so I stopped takin' the pills. But it was too late. D' y' know who

told me about . . . you . . . an' Linda . . . Your mother . . . she came to the factory and told me.

**Edward** Mickey, I don't know what she told you but Linda and I are just friends . . .

**Mickey** (*shouting for the first time*) Friends. I could kill you. We were friends weren't we? Blood brothers, wasn't it? Remember?

**Edward** Yes, Mickey, I remember.

**Mickey** Well, how come you got everything . . . an' I got nothin' (*Pause*) Friends. I've been thinkin' again Eddie. You an' Linda were friends when she first got pregnant, weren't y'?

**Edward** Mickey!

**Mickey** Does my child belong to you as well as everythin' else. Does she, Eddie, does she?

**Edward** (*shouting*) No, for God's sake!

*Pause*

*From the back of the auditorium we hear a Policeman through a loud hailer*

**Policeman 1** Now listen, son, listen to me; I've got armed marksmen with me. But if you do exactly as I say we won't need to use them, will we? Now look, Michael, put down the gun, just put the gun down, son.

**Mickey** (*dismissing their presence*) What am I doin' here Eddie? I thought I was gonna shoot y'. But I can't even do that. I don't even know if the thing's loaded.

*Mrs Johnstone slowly walks down the centre aisle towards the platform*

**Policeman 2** What's that woman doin'?

**Policeman 1** Get that woman away . . .

**Policeman 2** Oh Christ.

**Mrs Johnstone** Mickey. Mickey. Don't shoot him Mickey . . .

*Mickey contines to hold the gun in position*

**Mickey** Go away Mam . . . Mam you go away from here.

**Mrs Johnstone** No, son. (*She walks on to the platform*)

**Mickey** (*shouting*) Mam!

**Mrs Johnstone** Mickey. Don't shoot Eddie. He's your brother. You had a twin brother. I couldn't afford to keep both of you. His mother couldn't have kids. I agreed to give one of you away!

**Mickey** (*something that begins deep down inside him*) You! (*Screaming*) You! Why didn't you give me away! (*He stands glaring at her, almost uncontrollable with rage*) I could have been . . . I could have been him!

*On the word "him" Mickey waves at Edward with his gun hand. The gun explodes and blows Edward apart. Mickey turns to the Police screaming the word "No". They open fire and four guns explode, blowing Mickey away*

*Linda runs down the aisle*

*The Police are heard through the loud hailer*

Nobody move, please. It's all right, it's all over, just stay where you are.

## Music 37: Tell Me It's Not True

*As the Light on the scene begins to dim we see the Narrator spotlit, watching*

**Narrator**            And do we blame superstition for what came to pass?
                        Or could it be what we, the English, have come to know
                           as class?
                        Did you ever hear the story of the Johnstone twins,
                        As like each other as two new pins,
                        How one was kept and one given away,
                        How they were born, and they died, on the self same day?

**Mrs Johnstone**       Tell me it's not true,
   (*singing*)          Say it's just a story.
                        Something on the news
                        Tell me it's not true.
                        Though it's here before me,
                        Say it's just a dream,
                        Say it's just a scene
                        From an old movie of years ago,
                        From an old movie of Marilyn Monroe.
                        Say it's just some clowns,
                        Two players in the limelight,
                        And bring the curtain down.
                        Say it's just two clowns,
                        Who couldn't get their lines right,
                        Say it's just a show
                        On the radio,
                        That we can turn over and start again,
                        That we can turn over; it's only a game.

**Company**             Tell me it's not true,
                        Say I only dreamed it,
                        And morning will come soon.
                        Tell me it's not true,
                        Say you didn't mean it,
                        Say it's just pretend,
                        Say it's just the end,
                        Of an old movie from years ago
                        Of an old movie with Marilyn Monroe.

CURTAIN

# FURNITURE AND PROPERTY LIST

Only essential properties, as mentioned in the text, are listed here. Further dressing may be used at the Director's dicretion, but please see Production Note on page vi
Bomb—condom filled with water **(Sammy)**

## ACT I

**Mrs Lyons House:**
Furniture: table, settee, chair
Cushions
Bible and dictionary on bookcase
Mirror
Shopping bags

**Later:**
Cot
Child's shoes
Glass of whisky (for **Policeman**)

**Off stage:**
Striped apron, crate **(Milkman 1)**
Brush, dusters, mop bucket **(Mrs Johnstone)**
Parcel containing shoes **(Mrs Lyons)**
Listening funnel **(Gynaecologist)**
Two bundles **(Nurses)**
Pram **(Mrs Johnstone)**
Consumer goods **(Debt Collectors)**
Padding, including shawl **(Mrs Lyons)**
Toy gun **(Mrs Lyons)**
Catapult **(Mickey)**
Cap guns **(Children)**
Gun ("**Elliot Ness**")
Bazooka **(Sammy)**
Grenade ("**Sergeant**")
Bomb—condom filled with water **(Sammy)**
Air pistol **(Mickey)**
Parcel containing gun **(Edward)**
Letter **(Mrs Johnstone)**
Battered suitcase **(Mrs Johnstone)**
Furniture **(Johnstone children)**
Picture of the Pope **(Mrs Johnstone)**

**Personal:**
**Mrs Johnstone:** locket
**Mr Lyons:** pipe, wallet containing money
**Mickey:** pen knife

**Edward:** bag of sweets
**Sammy:** gun, handful of soil

## ACT II

**Classroom:**
Desks
Chairs
**Johnstone house:**
Kitchen equipment, including knife in a drawer
**Mickey's house**
Chest of drawers
Telephone

**Off stage:**
Rifle range gun **(Rifle range man)**
Coconut **(Rifle range man)**
Camera **(Linda)**
Handbag **(Mrs Johnstone)**
Hat **(Mrs Johnstone)**
Cards **(Mr Lyons)**
Shopping bags **(Linda)**
Pills **(Mickey)**
Mickey's working things **(Linda)**

**Personal:**
**Conductor:** tickets, money bag
**Mickey:** money
**Linda:** money. *Later:* high-heels; handbag containing pills
**Sammy:** knife, gun
**Mrs Lyons:** paper
**Mrs Johnstone:** overall
**Edward:** money

# LIGHTING PLOT

Composite set. Various interior and exterior settings

## ACT I

*To open:* Spot on Narrator

| | | |
|---|---|---|
| *Cue* 1 | As final moments of play are re-enacted<br>*Spotlight on replay* | (Page 1) |
| *Cue* 2 | After final moments have been re-enacted<br>*Revert to general lighting* | (Page 1) |
| *Cue* 3 | As scene segues to Mrs Lyons' house<br>*Crossfade to Lyons house* | (Page 3) |
| *Cue* 4 | As **Mrs Johnstone** goes to her house with babies<br>*Crossfade to Johnstone house* | (Page 9) |
| *Cue* 5 | **Mrs Johnstone:** "I've got to go to work."<br>*Crossfade to Lyons house* | (Page 11) |
| *Cue* 6 | At end of Music 11<br>*Crossfade to Johnstone house* | (Page 14) |
| *Cue* 7 | At end of Music 12<br>*Crossfade to Lyons house* | (Page 20) |
| *Cue* 8 | **Mrs Lyons:** "... my beautiful, beautiful son."<br>*Crossfade to street scene. Lyons "garden" still lit* | (Page 22) |
| *Cue* 9 | **Mrs Lyons:** "Frightened of ..."<br>*Fade to spot on Mrs Lyons* | (Page 28) |
| *Cue* 10 | At end of Music 16<br>*Crossfade to children in park* | (Page 28) |
| *Cue* 11 | Three children exit<br>*Crossfade to Johnstone house* | (Page 29) |
| *Cue* 12 | At end of Music 17<br>*Crossfade to Lyons house* | (Page 30) |
| *Cue* 13 | **Edward** leaves his house<br>*Crossfade to Johnstone house* | (Page 31) |
| *Cue* 14 | **Edward** leaves Johnstone house<br>*Crossfade to Lyons house* | (Page 32) |
| *Cue* 15 | At end of Music 18<br>*Crossfade to Johnstone house* | (Page 34) |

ACT II

*To open:* General lighting

# EFFECTS PLOT

See also Vocal Score for effects made by the Band

## ACT I

*Cue* 1    As heartbeat reaches maximum    (Page 9)
*Crying babies. Stop when ready*

*Cue* 2    As creditors leave with goods    (Page 10)
*Babies cry gently. Stop when ready*

*Cue* 3    **Mickey** fires air pistol    (Page 28)
*Sound of shot*

*Cue* 4    **Edward** fires air pistol    (Page 29)
*Sound of shot*

*Cue* 5    **Linda** fires air pistol    (Page 29)
*Metalic ping*

Repeat cues 3–5 when ready

## ACT II

*Cue* 6    **Neighbour:** "... shot of you rat bag."    (Page 37)
*Dog barks*

*Cue* 7    **Conductor** rings bells    (Page 39)
*Bell rings*

*Cue* 8    As **Linda** fires gun    (Page 52)
*Three shots*

*Cue* 9    **Mickey** is left alone    (Page 58)
*Christmas bells*

*Cue* 10    **Sammy:** "...fuckin' touch that ... Listen."    (Page 62)
*Alarm bell, explosion*

*Cue* 11    **Mickey** waves at Edward with the gun    (Page 69)
*Gun fires*

*Cue* 12    Police open fire    (Page 69)
*Four guns shoot*